# BUILDING SOCIALISM
# FIGHTING FASCISM

The RPB would like to thank Mahnaz Badihian,
Lisbit Bailey, Diego De Leo and Gregory Pond
for their particular support for this publication.
— The Editors

# BUILDING SOCIALISM
# FIGHTING FASCISM

Revolutionary Poets Brigade

Edited by
Jack Hirschman
John Curl
Lisbit Bailey

Copyright © 2021 by Kallatumba Press.
Edited by Jack Hirschman, John Curl, and Lisbit Bailey
All rights reserved. No part of this book may be reproduced by any means, including information storage and retrieval or photocopying, except for short excerpts in critical articles, without written permission of the publisher. Intellectual property reverts back to the individual poets and translators upon publication.
ISBN: 978-0-938392-15-6

Kallatumba Press
858A Union Street
San Francisco, CA 94133

http://revolutionarypoetsbrigade.org/
Printed in the United States of America.

# CONTENTS

PREFATORY

RAZU ALAUDDIN *(Bangladesh)* ... 10
AMPARO M. C. ALCONADA *(Argentina)* ... 12
INDRAN AMIRTHANAYAGAM *(Sri Lanka)* ... 14
ADRIAN ARIAS *(Peru)* ... 16
AYO AYOOLA-AMALE *(Nigeria)* ... 18
MAHNAZ BAHIDIAN *(USA/Iran)* ... 20
LISBIT BAILEY ... 22
LYNNE BARNES ... 24
VIRGINIA BARRETT ... 26
BENGT BERG *(Sweden)* ... 28
LINCOLN BERGMAN ...30
JUDITH AYN BERNHARD ... 32
SCOTT BIRD ... 34
CHARLES CURTIS BLACKWELL ... 35
VICTORIA BRILL ... 37
DANIEL BROOKS ... 38
KRISTINA BROWN ... 39
NEELI CHERKOVSKI ... 42
BOBBY COLEMAN ... 43
KITTY COSTELLO ... 44
JOHN CURL ... 45
GARY DANIEL *(Haiti)* ... 48
DIEGO DE LEO ... 50
CAROL DENNEY ... 51
CARLOS RAÚL DUFFLAR ... 53
MARIA ESTRADA ... 58
AGNETA FALK ... 60
MARCO FAZZINI *(Italy)* ... 62
MARCOS DE SOUSA FREITAS *(Brazil)* ... 64
RAFAEL JESÚS GONZÁLEZ *(USA/Mexico)* ... 66
ART GOODTIMES ... 70
ADAM GOTTLIEB ... 72
EGON GÜNTHER (Germany) ... 74

BILL HATCH ... 78
MARTIN HICKEL ... 79
JACK HIRSCHMAN ... 81
EVERETT HOAGLAND ... 84
BRUCE ISAACSON ... 87
SUSU JEFFREY ... 88
ZIBA KARBASSI *(Iran)* ... 90
DAVID LERNER ... 94
ANNA LOMBARDO *(Italy)* ... 98
KIRK LUMPKIN ... 102
devorah major ... 103
ELIZABETH MARINO ... 105
ÁNGEL L. MARTÍNEZ ... 106
KAREN MELANDER-MAGOON ... 107
SARAH MENEFEE ... 108
TUREEDA MIKELL ... 110
GAIL MITCHELL ... 115
WARDELL MONTGOMERY, JR. ... 116
ALEJANDRO MURGUÍA ... 119
MAJID NAFICY ... 121
CARMEN NARANJO *(Costa Rica)* ... 126
BILL NEVINS ... 128
CARLO PARCELLI ... 133
JERRY PENDERGAST ... 137
GREGORY POND ... 139
JEANNE POWELL ... 140
MIKE PULCAN ... 142
JUAN HERNÁNDEZ RAMÍREZ *(Mexico)* ... 144
FERNANDO RENDÓN *(Colombia)* ... 148
LEW ROSENBAUM ... 152
VINCENT ROMERO ... 155
GABRIEL ROSENSTOCK *(Ireland)* ... 156
SANDRO SARDELLA *(Italy)* ... 158
LUIS FELIPE SARMENTO *(Portugal)* ... 162
KIM SHUCK ... 164
DINO SIOTIS *(Greece)* ... 166
SANDRO SPINAZZI *(Italy)* ... 168

DOREEN STOCK ... 172
MATTHEW TALEBI ... 174
RAYMOND NAT TURNER ... 175
DAVID VOLPENDESTA ... 176
CATHLEEN WILLIAMS ... 178
NELLIE WONG ... 179
ANDRENA ZAWINSKI ... 181

BIOGRAPHIC NOTES ... 183

**VISUAL ARTISTS**

Front Cover: "Red Carnation" by Agneta Falk
Back Cover: "Born in Prison" by Mahnaz Badihian
Cover Design by Scott Bird
P. 26: Alex Mildrovich, "Cops"
P. 60: Victoria Brill, "Pandemonium"
P. 88: Yorkshire Collective, "Work"
P. 97: Yorkshire Collective, "In Between Truth and Lies"
P. 142: Alex Mildrovich, "Sleep"
P. 155: Alex Mildrovich, "Cash"
P. 164: Alex Mildrovich, "Blind"

**PREFATORY**

This is the second anthology from the Revolutionary Poets Brigade titled Building Socialism, with the subtitle, Fighting Fascism. Many of these poems were written over the last year, during which the coronavirus pandemic has exposed the heartlessness of fascism, and continues to do so. Here, the poets express thoughts and feelings, dreams and nightmares, questions and answers. Perspectives and languages range from local to international. The themes are universal: human rights, immigration, homelessness, tyranny of the military and the police, and senseless murders of the young, black and brown among us. Consider these poems a call to thoughtful and loving action to rescue the future for all.

As editors of this anthology, we have recognized that fascism is growing not only in the United States, and that the need for building socialism is not just an American need, which is why those two themes are reflected in no fewer than 10 languages in this book. They are: the Bangla of Bangladesh, Italian, Haitian Creole, Portuguese (from both Portugal and Brazil), Greek, Nahuatl (of Mexico), German, Spanish, English (as distinguished from American) and the American language as well. We have welcomed the internationalization of the two themes, and their variations, because only an international working-class of socialist progressivity can bring about the achievement of socialist and communist dreaming and the destruction of the fascism that is pervading and pillaging the good people of this blood-soaked world.

Editors
Jack Hirschman, John Curl, Lisbit Bailey

**BUILDING SOCIALISM
FIGHTING FASCISM**

**RAZU ALAUDDIN (Bangladesh)**

আমেরিকা, তুমি শ্বাস নিতে পারছ তো?

তুমি বলেছিলে শ্বাস নিতে পারছ না;
কিন্তু পুলিশ সে-কথা আমলে নেয়নি।
যেন ওই সাদা হাঁটুর চাপে কালোরা মোটেও মরে না-
কালোরা এতই অদম্য আর এতই শক্তিশালী!

তোমার যে-শ্বাস,আর চিৎকার, আর যত গোঙ্গানি-
সব ছেড়ে দিয়ে তুমি চলে গেলে, সাদা করোনার চেপে-ধরা
শ্বাসরোধে।
আমরা এখন তোমারই শ্বাস, চিৎকার আর গোঙ্গানি হয়ে ছড়িয়ে
পড়েছি
রাস্তায়, আর শহরে শহরে, প্রতিটি রাজ্যে। আমেরিকা ছেড়ে
আরও দূর দেশে দেশে।
কালো ভাই, তুমি চলে গিয়ে ফিরে
এলে অদম্য রূপে।

আমেরিকা,তুমি শ্বাস নিতে পারছ তো?
৩১-০৫-২০২০

## RAZU ALAUDDIN (Bangladesh)

## AMERICA, CAN YOU BREATHE?

You complained you couldn't breathe;
but the police did not seem to notice.
As if blacks are never strangled under those white knees—
As if blacks are so invincible and mighty!

You left us bringing an end to
all your respiration, screaming and moaning
because of the white-Corona attack
We all now are metamorphosed into
your respiration, screaming and moaning
and spread all over the streets,
from one city to another, and in every state.
We've gone beyond America and reached countries far off.
Black brother, you left us
yet you're back invincibly!

America, can you breathe?

*(Translated from Bangla by Abdus Selim)*

## AMPARO CASABELLAS ALCONADA (Argentina)

### FRATERNA TIERRA

se alzarán al fin las manos de la edad
cronológicamente desatarán el nudo
de tu garganta
hermano muerto escupiré los látigos
hermano mío gritaré que has vivido
donde se esconde la masacre
con tus manos presas del castigo
fundaré las calles que bautizaron tu destierro
del eco de un vestigio de tu voz
rescataré la libertad que hemos dormido
naciendo naciéndonos cada día
comprenderemos que nos sobran las fronteras
que desconsoladamente nos han robado los abrazos.

## AMPARO CASABELLAS ALCONADA (Argentina)

## FRATERNAL LAND

in the end the hands of our age
will raise themselves date by date
will untie the knot of your throat
my dead brother I will spit out the lashes
I will shout that you have lived
where the massacre was hidden
with your hands in chains
I will found the streets that baptized your exile
from the echo of a vestige of your voice. I will
ransom the liberty that has been put to sleep, being
born, giving birth to us each day—
we shall understand that we have too many borders
that have heartbreakingly stolen our embraces.

*(Translated from Spanish by Marcelo Holot
and Doreen Stock)*

## INDRAN AMIRTHANAYAGAM (Sri Lanka)

### HAITI, NOU LA
### (We Are With You)

In what language shall I cry
basta. Enough. Arrete.
Which of these do you favor,
or shall I scream in esperanto
to be fair to everyone
and none of us? Bus drivers
and passengers are afraid
in Haiti. Swatches of key
roads are patrolled by gangs
in search of money and
people to ferret away into
their lairs, to demand ransom,
to grow fat with power
and dominion, with marksmen
smart and wily, able to defend
their territory. Goodbye law
and order. Goodbye the pacific
life where everybody believes
in dominion of laws, right, justice--
fucked by the plastic-ridden beach,
by love gone south, and words
that do not make wounds disappear,
just cover them up. Band aid.
Raise awareness. Play music
and write poems. We will build
back better. Butter slop. Rubbish.
Bring in foreign troops, full-
court press, in body armor.
Go into no man's land. Kill,
be killed. Escobar. Bonnie
and Clyde. Jesse James. Name
the outlaw. Fight the outlaw.

Fire on fire. With music. Bring
in wailers, funeral marchers
after all is finished. Don't ever
forget. We love you Haiti
to death, more than death.

## ADRIAN ARIAS (Perú)

**8:46**

(respirar con intención agitada)
Es difícil ser un ángel, pero se aprende.
La bota del policía sofocando el cuello
parece la primera instrucción para convertirse en ángel
¿Pero quiero ser ángel?
Alguien tomó la decisión por mi.
(respiración larga y pausada)
Es doloroso convertirse en ángel
el escalofrío en el pecho parece interminable.
Cuando eres un ángel puedes sentir el dolor de otros
a veces el dolor pesa más que una montaña
más que el cielo y las estrellas.
(respiración más tranquila)
Me alivia saber que hay gente despertando
y luchando para evitar que más botas de policías traten de
                                   convertir en ángeles
a cada persona de color, a cada persona diferente
Nos matan porque no quieren escucharnos
nos matan por una rabia ancestral que ni ellos mismos
                                   entienden.
(respiración apurada)
Cuando eres un ángel estás en todos lados y en ninguno
escuchando los reclamos los llantos los gritos
entre los destellos de luz azul y roja, allí
puedes ayudar a que otros respiren mejor.
Es difícil ser un ángel, pero con tiempo, se aprende.
(respiración larga y final)

\* 8:46 se refiere al tiempo que George Floyd fue sofocado por un policia hasta morir.

**ADRIAN ARIAS (Peru)**

**8:46 ***

(breathe with agitated intention)
It's hard to be an angel, but you learn.
The policeman's boot suffocating the neck
seems the first instruction to become an angel
But do I want to be an angel?
Someone made the decision for me.
(long breath)
It is painful to become an angel
the chill in my chest seems endless.
When you are an angel you can feel the pain of others
sometimes the pain weighs more than a mountain
more than the sky and the stars.
(calmer breathing)
I am relieved to know that there are people waking up
and fighting to stop more police boots from trying to turn
                                                                    into angels
to each person of color, to each different person.
They kill us because they don't want to listen to us
they kill us because of an ancestral rage that they
                                       themselves don't understand.
(hurried breathing)
When you are an angel you are everywhere and nowhere
listening to the claims, the cries, the screams
Between the flashes of blue and red light, there
you can help others breathe easier.
It is difficult to be an angel, but with time, you learn.
(long, final breath.

* 8:46 refers to the time George Floyd was being suffocated by the police until he died.

*(Translated from Spanish by the Author)*

## AYO AYOOLA-AMALE (Nigeria)

### THE FACES OF EVIL

We watch power corruption make system fool,
everything is rigged pretty much scot-free.
Fascism gives birth, navel including
a chance to exploit the body they shot brutally a chance to
                                          make the world their throne
giving decayed milk to the have-nots, the wall,
the stench of decayed minds hall,
of leaders, riding horses, leading poverty, meanly true,
of people becoming horses and carts for all time, corruptly
                                                                  cruel.
Strikes at the heart of why we mean like fallen dry leaves,
                                                                  eroding.
Collecting tax from a table top trader but exempting the
haves. Kingmakers desire to be fed with the morsel
which fell from the king's table.

We watch power corruption make system fool,
makes state cut the sun, gloom and lazy
with both its eyes, vision hazy.
Corruption attacking the cat and the lion,
the only one sound's the weep,
rats bend to left and right,
bend to greed in dark rooms.
Even poets are illegal like cocaine.
These fascists conscience tumbles down in a hasty flowing
                                                   river, for convenience
totally consumed by self, it trips over hard rock, obscurity.
Possessions living in a balloon become an obsession.
These fascists trade on rules in the sky, earn evil gold,
                                                        unknown pleasure
their indifference leaps up to the tearing shoulders of the
                                                                     people,
betray peace barely crawling, a presence.

We watch power corruption make system fool,
menace has gained flesh into their backbones
frightening to the people, like an antelope close by a
                              famished lion.
The immortal mind winks
at you all impotent pacifist
who insist the need is the need, that grew old
yet we live in a world that
lives in us like the corn earworms
lives and feeds on the silk of the corn.
The world lives with us like moth on leaf hairs.
Fascism's feet too long breathing,
ran into our bedroom and hide in a space under the bed,
so anytime they choose; they can squeeze and sponge
our blood dry to feed their mutilated heart, struck blind.

## MAHNAZ BADIHIAN (USA/Iran)

## WHO SAID AMIRI IS DEAD?
*For Amiri Baraka*

Who said Amiri is dead and
no longer will write poems like "Who Blew up America?"
Those who caused bloodshed in The Middle East?
Those who caused millions of people
To leave their motherland and die in strange lands?
Those whose I.D. cards list the worst human abuse
In history: slavery.

Who, who said Amiri is dead?
Who, who, who?
Those who got rich and more prosperous from killing
Innocent people across the World?
Or those who killed robbing nations
Of their best and brightest minds?
Those who talk about democracy all the time, and
Become close allies of backward,
Undemocratic rich Saudi Amirs and hate Fidel?
Those who overthrew the democratically elected,
Educated, nationalist Mosaddegh from Iran
And helped the fanatic clergy grab power
To ruin the ancient, rich Persian culture?

Who said Amiri is dead
Who, who, who?
Those who did not like Amiri's hostility towards white
                                          society?
Those who kicked red poet Jack Hirschman out of UCLA
Only because he had humanistic antiwar ideas?
Those who serve the interests of banks over people
And kick poor people out of their homes?
Those who killed tens of thousands
of Africans and Iraqis, by fabricating lies.

Who said Amiri is dead?
Who, who, who?
Those who have so much money wipe their ass with it
while every day countless kids suffer
from malnutrition and lack of food,
even in America?
Those who are openly or secretly racist?
Those who killed Malcolm X and placed a bullet
In innocent Oscar Grant's head?

Who said Amiri is dead?
Who, who, who?
Those who never read Amiri's poems and
Never understood pain in black poetry?
Those who never looked at those big,
protesting eyes on Amiri's face?
Who said Amiri cannot be a poet laureate because
He does not shut his mouth
They must learn that Amiri will not die
He will only recycle between pages of world poetry
in the heart of revolutionaries
in the anthologies of protest poetries
Amiri will go on to live and recycle!

Who said Amiri is dead?
Who, who, who?

**LISBIT BAILEY**

**FLOWERS OF ZEUS**

These aren't flowers
for beaus' boutonnières,
mothers' bouquets,
doctors' altruism,
or presidential luck.

These flowers of Zeus
rise from roots
alive underground.
They are never dormant.

Workers' hands and faces
reddened by their labor as
they scrape and scratch a living
from under capitalism's thumb.

Red expressions of pain
before crimson rises or
like unearthed passion
compelling us to live lovingly.

Carnation is a word of honor.
Standing for blood embodied,
for remembering and celebrating
the people's sacrifices.

The people of Portugal
toppled their capitalist city.
Ended the dictatorship
by peaceful reincarnation.

The Red Carnation is the joy
of the Portuguese people who are

the midwives of their democracy.
A community tested and now evolved.

On April 25th, let's emulate
the wakened power
of the Portuguese people as
we raise red carnations everywhere.

## LYNNE BARNES

### OSCAR DANIEL'S EYES*
*There is currently one state that has made at least
the weak beginnings of a better order.*
                *—Adolf Hitler, 1920s*

Five score and nine years ago,
Forsyth County, Georgia,
began its purge,
ripping Black people from its land*
by lynching, kangaroo courts,
by nightriders burning homes, terrorizing.

Leave or die.

Like an invading army,
white people planted their flags
on these lands.
The names on the deeds
were all white names
after seven years of taxes paid.

Across the Atlantic,
young Hitler turns twenty-three.

In this year 1912,
Azzie Crow and her family—
seven-year-old Bonnie,
18-month-old Esta,
among them—
watch Oscar Daniel
slam from a scaffold,
land in the air inches
above their feet, dangle,
strangle for eleven minutes,
as five thousand witness
from the arena-like
hillsides around them.

This Black teen was arrested,
convicted too quickly,
too thinly,
of raping and murdering
Azzie's daughter, Mae.

His cell mate
died before the trial—
bullets to the body,
sledgehammer
to the skull
by a jail-crashing mob.

In 1952, Azzie revealed
a memory
haunting her psyche
for forty years—
Oscar Daniel's boyish,
innocent eyes
locking with hers

in those opening moments
of Forsyth County's
fear-and-hate-frenzied
white supremacist
embrace of racial cleansing,

its Jim Crow rage
into a fire-scarred,
rope-frayed,
bullet-holed
three-dimensional
blood-soaked blueprint

telegraphed across the sea,
and improved, improved,
in unimaginable ways.

\* There were 1,098 Black people living in Forsyth Country,
Georgia in 1912. Within a matter of months, it had dropped to 30

**COPS**
**Alex Mildrovich**

## VIRGINIA BARRETT

## WHAT IS NEEDED

They are razing the old hospital. What a
racket. A woman outside keeps screaming,

"Shut the fuck up!" but not at jackhammers
(those indomitable drills, drilling) . . . "just

crazy," we'd say. The old poinsettia is starting
to sprout red leaves; ancient Aztec medicine,

here a holiday display, wild varieties disappear
to deforestation. Beside me, Kahlo stares

full-blown from the cover of Fine Arts. Her
scarlet lips dying to swear, she demands

to know who stuck her there. A communist
turned into a commodity—cabrona!—and

the museum shop features a fair trade Frida
doll, like a small effigy to burn. The new

Sutter Health releases homeless addicts
from Emergency after minimal care. "Shut

the fuck up! Shut the fuck up!" toward
the graffitied park. "What is needed to write

good poems about the outward world," the poet
said, "is inwardness." Sometimes our introspection

turns too obscure . . . maybe just sit and listen?
Quiet now, how loud this peace we need.

## BENGT BERG (Sweden)

### De nödvändiga frågorna

När hon säger, vi säger, du, de …
när hon säger sång säger du marsch
när hon säger regnbåge säger du bunker
när hon säger sol och gryning säger du nattmörker
när hon säger att det är möjligt att respektera också svaghet
säger du att det bara finns plats för dem som är starka
när hon frågar sig själv var den stora glädjen finns
säger du att den finns i natten, i svarta mörkret
när hon frågar var du hittar detta mörker
säger du att det kommer av sig själv
när hon frågar hur det är möjligt
svarar du att det måste vara
möjligt för annars skulle
inte fascismen vara
möjlig!
Hon frågar vem är det
som gör fascismen möjlig
och hon får inget svar, men
vi vet svaret: kapitalet, de som
aldrig skulle riskera sina privilegier
för några ynka människors skull, det pågår
hela tiden en normalisering av landningsbanan,
manegen krattas medan orättvisorna djupnar och
arbetslösheten och rekryteringen till den underjordiska
källaren bara fortsätter; intet är nytt under solen!

Men det finns motstånd, mod, beslutsamhet och de som vill ta kampen: "Bara så blir människan människa, genom att vara människa!"

Citatet är ur en dikt av Otto René Castillo, från Guatemala, som deltog i frihetskampen på 1960-talet och torterades och döades av diktaturen.

**BENGT BERG (Sweden)**

**THE ESSENTIAL QUESTIONS**

When she says, we say, you, them…
when she says song you say march
when she says rainbow you say bunker
when she says sun and dawn you say darkness of night
when she says it's possible to also respect weakness
you say there's only a place for those who are strong
when she asks herself where the big joy exists
you say it can be found in the night, in the black darkness
when she asks where do you find this darkness
you say it happens by itself
when she asks how it's possible
you answer it has to be
possible otherwise how
would fascism be
possible!
She asks who makes fascism possible
and she gets no answer, but
we know the answer: capital, those who
never would give up their privileges
for some wretched people's sake, it goes on
all the time, a normalization like a landing-strip
setting the stage while injustices deepen and unemployment
and recruitment in secret cellars just continue,
nothing new under the sun!

But there's resistance, courage, determination by those who want
to take the fight on: "A human being becomes a human being,
by being a human being!"

*(Translated from Swedish by Agneta Falk)*

*The quote is from a poem by Otto René Castillo, from Guatemala, who took part in the freedom fight in 1960s and was tortured to death by the dictatorship there.*

# LINCOLN BERGMAN

## A WAY OF SPEAKING

Speak secretly
Because the walls have ears.
Secretly, as in love
And revolution.

Actions test of truth
And bravery in act
Not in reckless words
On surveilled mobile phones.

A revolutionary takes chances
When chances must be taken
A chance at any other time
Is perhaps to waste a life,

Perhaps many lives.
And a revolutionary
Treasures life so much
He, or she, is willing to give it.

Does it aid your ego
To boast of plans already made
Or give away a confidence
Or speak of who you saw with whom?

Remember,
As you speak
You may be endangering
The one you tell.

"There will be
No more pain

If you tell us
The names."

Always speak
What is necessary for success
Too much, too often, too soon
Guarantees failure.

These are the times
When the fist of fascism closes
But we also have our fists
And the work-hardened muscle of history.

The peoples of the earth
Are with us
So our cautions
Do not come from fear.

In spite of our mistakes
Divisions and despairs
We have not acquiesced
We have begun to learn resistance.

Do not be afraid to act.
Act with the energy of an occupied nation.
The energy of knowing you have
One more day outside the concentration camps.

Expansion yields protection
Explain, persuade, and organize
Do not be afraid to learn
Ways to speak to the needs of the people.

## JUDITH AYN BERNHARD

## FORBEARERS

1947
A baseball player, a Negro Leagues
infielder who had faced court-martial
in the army for refusing to move to the
back of a bus, became the first Black
to play in the Major Leagues and Oh,
did they torture and harass him. But
Jackie Robinson never lost his dignity.

1959
A basketball player, one of the best,
boycotted a game in the American
South because he and other Black
Minnesota Lakers were denied
rooms and service and Oh, it
wasn't a popular decision. But
Elgin Baylor never relented.

1966
A good-looking man, a boxer, told
the world he was "The Greatest"
(He was.) but when he stood up for
his religion, his name change, Oh,
they came down hard on him. But
Muhammad Ali never wavered.

1968
Two Olympic runners, among the
fastest in the world, raised their
black-gloved fists in protest as
The Star Spangled Banner played
and Oh, it cost them plenty. But
Tommie Smith and John Carlos
never recanted or backed down.

Remember their names now and forever
and add the names of athletes they
inspired to stand up (or kneel) and
speak out, to insist on justice no
matter the consequences.
Remember: Arthur Ashe, Jim Brown,
Larry Doby, Bill Russell, Kareem
Abdul Jabbar, Mahmoud Abdul-Rauf
Bubba Wallace, Colin Kaepernick,
LaBron James, and other NBA players.

And WMBA players and other women
athletes and players in nearly every
sport around the world who wear
BLACK LIVES MATTER on shirts.

Tell everyone about them!

**SCOTT BIRD**

**CHILDREN OF A WHITMAN DAHLIA**

I am a red dahlia
a Mexican Daisy growing
budding from the crown
of my own head & tanglehair

You pluck the red blossom
and pin it to your lapel
above the dangling Lenin broadside
and proud hammer-sickle swinging

We remember carnations, roses
and other red proses infinite
in their strength when
taped to the tip of a razor fountain pen

Fight by the cover of the dark word night for
joy is an upward struggle
a radical bow and arrow of lip
and tongue flexing into smile

Fascism can only frown, its porous heart
soaked and drowned in the blind glaze
of power's greed and greed's power needs only
to read your lips and remember the word

*Always,* we have it within
ourselves to disassemble all factions
today and in the first word of the first line
of every stanza written in our poems

I
you  we
     —children of Whitman's Best Dahlia—
fight fascism
*always.*

## CHARLES CURTIS BLACKWELL

## GETTIN' DOWN TO THE ROOT, THE DEEP ROOT OF IT

In the colonies
tobacco leaves
were once used as a currency
no use pretending, America, the ism ain't here
Rope manufactured; Cotton was king
supply and demand; mass production
Get it while you can
January white-sheet sale
Days of slavery, she a white woman gave
birth to a dark baby
Massa murdered the baby and her too
Gypsy moss hangs lowly.

Swirling clouds of tobacco smoke
hand-rolled cigarette, greasy greenish cap
on head
Confederate pasted on window; lottery tickets
sold here, candy bars, cigarettes
Nowhere near the Mason Dixon line
neighbor one pumps over gazes at Black man;
pump registers full tank of gas
"Hi, how's it going?"
"Fine," the Black man replies while finishing
a candy bar and pumping gas
This white fellow speaking even though
there's a klan uniform in his back seat
neatly folded
station owner puts cigarette out, then
places 3 fingers outside pants pocket
greeting fellow klansman.

Loyalty to the royal family/with tons of wealth
for economics is the issue,
Supply and Demand.

Badges manufactured, bully clubs, pistols,
bullets and hard liquor
Currency in England referred to as pounds;
ism with royalty attached
The baby's going to be born dark
Now they must calculate the cost
of how much the rope weighs

## VICTORIA BRILL

## DONT SWALLOW

dont swallow nuttin you cant pronounce
no malthusian luciferian beelzebubs
no trilateral intermonetarian funded packages
no algorithms memes or bots
no nuclear submarines
no crypto elastico dioxy blather
just tutti frutti all the way

dont chew on no isms or schisms
no matter how nuanced
contextualized
financialized
past your eyes
homo gen ized
no bio engineered genetically modified nuttin
no gmo's no cafo's
no WTO's no WHO's no Davos
nutting fast nuttin to go
just tutti frutti all the day.

## DANIEL BROOKS

## ESSENTIAL IS CODE FOR DISPOSABLE

We are lambs
We are cattle
We are flesh
to be used
blood to be spilt
We are caretakers
We are preparers
each part to be
drained hacked & sold
We feed we clothe
We nurture we educate
We cook We serve we clean
We produce all things
We are the masses
We are the people
We are the workers
of the world
reimagining the world
one brush stroke at a time
blending its colors
on newspaper
and paper plates
create a world
where we care
for one another
where we own
what we produce
having only what we need.

## KRISTINA BROWN

## QR/CELEBRATION ELEGY

QR.
QR Hand.
He's gone now.
Wild and dignified
He was so great
So strong
So deeply sweet,
Always unrolling new rhythms
Making the sun shine brighter
the sky look bluer.

Oh, how I adored him!

Everyone did.
He made it easy.
Always ready with a kind word
or the right word
whatever your piece or your song
Whatever you needed.
Always generous
Always kind
Always full of empathy and sympathy,
                charity and clarity
So big hearted
filled with love and joy

Pouring out the words
Laying them on
Lifting us up.
He was
Free
jazz.

He was unexpected
sizzling psychedelia.

Most of you probably knew him too
even if he wasn't as famous as he deserved to be.

Confident but easy
Loving and kind
Have I said that before?
Not merely superficially nice
But deeply humane
Forgiving the bad
Celebrating the good.

He was
A mighty soul.
Not bent
Not crushed
by cruelty, injustice, and prejudice.
Working to make life better for everyone
He gave the gifts of respect and love.

I wasn't alone in my admiration.
Almost everyone who knew him loved him.
When I wrote this, I thought,
"If he ever did anything wrong,
I'll hear about it now."
But I haven't.
No one's said a bad word about him.
He was the sun rising
the espresso steaming
the tree blossoming,
Taken away by capitalism to Vallejo
then taken away
Altogether.

Joyful free

Always in the rhythm
on or off the beat
refusing to be circumscribed
To be less than amazing

Always so far out there always so close to the heart
to the bone.

QR
Bubbling
Riffing
Yelping with joy
Leaping to another plane
of existence

Carrying us with him.

QR
So wise and generous and ecstatic but sad sometimes too

Missing old friends who had gone before.

Now
QR
is gone too.

Oh! How we loved you!

How you loved us.

# NEELI CHERKOVSKI

## OF THE FAR RIGHT

In formal gardens they awaken
Like blossoming vines, white men,
Right men, men who road at night
Coveting hoods, hearts like cesspools

These men dine with Satan under
The capitol rotunda, men of
The New Reich find an enemy,
Small children locked in cages

They celebrate slow and determined
Starvation of the elderly poor,
They admire Adolf Hitler's ghost
Rising on death-camp minds

This is the Ku Klux Klan reborn,
Flag-bearers, cowards, Americans.

## BOBBY COLEMAN

## WHY WE STILL ASK

why we still ask, where is the love,
the real kind of love, that we give to ourselves
when we're connected, when we are taught
how our lives were once, before creatures lied,
and warred over trees, sat in the White House
and stormed the Capitol, encouraged by anglers
of mischief and madness; why we still ask,
where is the love, since the new Prez says
how the numbers roll back, but merely to W's,
that billionaires rock, if they share a few cents,
that we're losing the race so let's get tough
that we're in a trade war and have now had enough
so we ask again, why cancel love,
why wipe out art, not offer the class,
why turn the artroom into a sty
of STEMful dung and racial myopia,
missing the point, thumping our chests,
announcing ourselves, narcissoGAStically,
and why we still ask, where is the love,
is because of this: when we jilted the poet
and broke her heart, when we did that,
the whole simple reason for being together
for our full engagement, our knee at the altar,
our exchange of rings, was a lousy trick,
a mask was used, an imposter was paid,
a betrothal to fascism, not social love
and the only way out, since we still have to ask
is to return to the poem, our first Declaration
that we love each other, and will not sell the House
or the house of Whitman, Emerson, and Thoreau
and will marry in truth, and escape with our muse,
not the fake one still there, we have three ushers beaming,
giving proof through the night that our hearts are still free.

## KITTY COSTELLO

## TWO FIGHTING FASCISM ACROSTICS

F reeing ourselves from us-and-them
I deology would be a
G ood start.
H atred highjacks hearts.
T hat's its craft, so let's
I nspect the divide... carefully... again.
N o human is bad without a backstory. Let's
G o deeper to the root of wrongs. Let us

F eel and avert all heart-hardening and
A ttend beyond justified outrage,
S ee and tend to whatever needs breaking without be-
C oming shattered or cruel or gone.
I t's an alchemy of Warrior
S pirit as yet unseen.
M ake yourself a new kind of sword.

F or every child born
I nvited or not, of whatever creed and breed,
G rant each one their basic needs; thwart childhood
H arm, abuse, neglect—
T rauma that snarls itself into exponential grown-up
I nsanity, inhumanity doomed to repeat until
N one but the tone-deaf can hear
G ood people staying thunderously silent... again.

F rontload goodness. Bestow
A bundant blessings on each new
S elf arriving here, and upon their parents.
C ultivate humans who know what love
I s and is not and who know the
S ound of truth being spoken, the
M agic of harmony being sung.

## JOHN CURL

## THEY SHALL NOT PASS

> *Be loving enough to absorb evil and*
> *understanding enough to turn an enemy into a friend.*
> —*Martin Luther King, Jr.*

Downtown I walked along, a warm
night, everyone out, it was bustling,
women in colorful dresses, dogs
sniffing each other, children hopping
over the cracks in the sidewalk.

Then the street collapsed at my feet.
I staggered back. Lampposts, vehicles,
people cascading down into a vast pit,
falling, they were all disappearing into
darkness, I couldn't see bottom; from
the shadows belched fumes and
smoke. I was choking. I knew that to
breathe those toxic fumes meant death.

Then I awoke, shaken.

They say that the thoughts you
have right after a dream are really
part of the dream itself.

I thought about my grandfather,
an immigrant to America, of how
his dreams collapsed into the Great
Depression fascism World War 2.

Then suddenly I was downtown again.
From down the block, in the middle of
the street, women, men, children, a long
procession, all ages and descriptions,

colorfully dressed, carrying banners and
signs, chanting as they paraded toward me,
there were so many of them, they kept coming
and coming. As they approached, I realized
the signs and chant weren't in English,
but sounded familiar, I'd heard that chant
before, though I didn't recall from where.

Then I suddenly understood the words:
NO PASARÁN. THEY SHALL NOT PASS.

It was from the Spanish Civil War
of the 1930s, before World War 2. It
had been a rallying cry of the populace
defending Madrid against Franco's
fascists, brought back to America by
the Abraham Lincoln Brigade and other
international brigades of volunteers
fighting in Spain to stop fascism before
it engulfed all of Europe and the world.

As the line of marchers arrived at
where I stood on the edge of the sidewalk,
a woman at the front handed me a sign and,
without another thought, I stepped off the
curb and was swept into the march. I felt
exhilarated, striding side by side with them,
chanting:

NO PASARÁN. THEY SHALL NOT PASS

Then we stopped short.

The intersection was blocked by
men in black military gear with helmets,
shields, guns, truncheons, and behind
them a group in white robes, holding banners

painted with rune-like symbols. And
behind those were armored vehicles
and uniforms as far as I could see.
I wanted to get out of there fast, but
I was fixated, I couldn't move.
They started toward us.

Then I awoke again. I lay there a few
minutes thinking about my dream.

I wondered what my grampa
would think of the world now.

## GARY DANIEL (Haiti)

### SI ....

Si nanchon an pa ta janmen bliye
dezafi politisyen lage li.

Si nanchon an pa ta janmen bliye
se yon restavèk li te vote.

Si nanchon an pa ta janmen bliye
pil magouy zanmi li kadre pou li.

Si lajenès pa ta janmen vale
medsin kanyank kanyank k pare pou li

Si gran paran pa ta bobo nennenn
ak fo flanbo pou tiye lalin.

Si lagè avèti pa touye rèv pèp
Li pa t ap benyen nan tatalolo.

... Si..Si...li pa t a dèyè plimen lavi.

## GARY DANIEL (Haiti)

**IF...**

If the nation had never forgotten
his misfortune caused by these politicians;

If the nation had not realized
that she had voted a lackey president;

And if the nation could never erase
from his memory the traps set by his friends.

If the youths never swallowed
these remedies badly concocted for their future;

If our grandparents did not keep on kissing our godmothers
with their false torches to eclipse our moonlight;

If announcing a war does not kill the people's dreams;
the people can never get bogged down in fecal matter.

... If... if... the people would not fight that way to survive.

*(Translated from Haitian Creole by the Author)*

# DIEGO DE LEO

## REVOLT

We, who have lived and suffered
through an oppressive fascistic
government whose officials, under
the mantle of false pretense, stomp
on the defenseless while enriching
themselves, must now reveal that

an untold number of children are
going hungry, some never reaching
adulthood. This is nothing short of
a crime against humanity. The arms
dealers and insurance companies
have blood all over their hands.

History tells us that some poets who
spoke up against the tyrannies in their
times were imprisoned; others faced
the firing squad. Now it's up to the
the poets who've reached the limit
of tolerance to write and organize

a movement of revolt with the vigor
of a torrential river in order to untangle
this society from the tentacles of the
the ever repressive, growing fascism
behind the racism and hatreds that
feed the status quo its indifference.

**CAROL DENNEY**

**WE LOOKED LIKE FLOWERS**
*(capo5 use A key of D)*

we looked like flowers
when we were young
we looked like angels
every one
our skin was beautiful
our eyes were bright
we sleep in doorways now
night after night

asking for handouts
is no one's desire
makes you so small inside
makes you so tired
just have to roll along
whatever goes by
and want to surrender
and just want to die

we built all the bridges
we fought all the wars
now it's just sirens
the slamming of doors
the slamming of jail cells
again and again
once we were soldiers
once we were workers
now we're just them

they look at our clothing
they look at our shoes
our troubles and stories
are yesterday's news

if we were puppies
they'd throw us a bone
if we were children
they'd take us all home

wish I had wings
wish I could fly
make me a home somewhere
up in the sky
where nobody hates
where nobody stares
where somebody listens
where somebody cares


Chorus:
night after night
day after day
looking for mercy
to meet us halfway
they want us to leave
but where do we go
we are just people
they don't want to know

# CARLOS RAÚL DUFFLAR

## TO THE UNSUNG HEROES OF THE POOR PEOPLE'S CAMPAIGN: THE LONG MARCH CONTINUES

Distant memories poured in from the 60s inside of the belly of
                                                                the beast
The horrors of savage capitalism that surrounded our lives
Dog eats dog
Apartheid which defends fascism since it presents
The mask of colonialism of violence, of sickness, of hunger,
And the denial of human rights and justice with their holy mass
And a quote from Malcolm X – "Show me a capitalist and I'll
                                                        show you a bloodsucker"
We were a generation guided with love and peace and for
                                                         freedom now
Marching for peace and justice and democracy
Let a new Earth rise and let a new world be born on the ashes of
                                                   an uncivilized society
Let the future be written for the people and not the privileged
                                                         few
When some friends invited me to listen and to hear Martin
                                                         Luther King Jr
At the Riverside Church as we sat down surrounded by
                                                         thousands of people
When he spoke A Time to Break Our Silence Beyond Vietnam
It hit directly home how many sons of working class people
                                                         suffered
The heavy toll of body bags sent back to the communities around
                                                         the country
A bitter moment of weeping mothers that will never see their
                                                         sons again
The train of peace rolled on
On Spring Mobilization Against the War in Vietnam
We had gathered in Central Park bandshell
On April the 15th of 1967, Martin Luther King Jr, David
                                                         Dellinger,
and many others spoke against the effects of the war on the
                                                         people

A bright light shined when we were marching towards the front
                                    of the United Nations
Where the rally was
And singing, "Hey LBJ, how many children did you kill today?"
All things come on time
Where LBJ dropped out running for the second time as president
Eight months passed where Dr Martin Luther King Jr, Marian
                                    Wright Edelman,
and Stanley Levinson and the SCLC staff
When the PPC was born
It was a beautiful moment for the wretched of the Earth
And again Martin Luther King invited the Committee of 100
With the most exploited representatives of the poor workers in
                                    the country:
Indigenous, Blacks, Puerto Ricans, and poor whites from
Appalachia and allies
The nationally oppressed people rejoiced when he proclaimed an
Economic Bill of Rights, struggling against the boundless greed
And later they organized the nine regions around the country
To bring nine Caravans for the Long March on Washington, DC,
                                    with our demands
So when Martin Luther King Jr and the staff of SCLC in
solidarity with the sanitation workers
On strike for a living wage and starting the Poor People's
                                    Campaign
On our march to Washington, DC, to the seat of power
The enemies of humanity struck a brutal assassination of Dr
                                    Martin Luther King Jr
6:01 on April the 4th of 1968
I saw it with my own eyes the people rebel – over a hundred
                                    went in flames
Three weeks later, the SCLC had a meeting and elected Ralph
                                    Abernathy as president
The Poor People's Campaign would go forward later
And a month passed and Coretta Scott King led the Mother's
                                    Day March in Washington, DC
Of the Poor People's Campaign and the opening of Resurrection
                                    City
With 5000 women down the half-torn city with a rally

With the National Welfare Rights Organization and New York
                                                                Welfare Rights Association
To restore the benefits that were cut of child care, Head Start and
                                                                       food stamps
and an end to the war in Vietnam
The time is right to do right
When the New York headquarters of the Poor People's Embassy
                                                 and the Poor People's Campaign
Hit the pavement organizing all over the city with rallies and
                                                     community meetings
Calling on people to join when I joined
The time is coming when the Northeastern Caravan would arrive
                                                             from Boston
To pick us up as we all gathered on 142nd Street and 7th Avenue
To march down and meet the East Harlem Puerto Rican
                                                               Contingent
And march down to Fifth Avenue to rally at the Bandshell in
                                                               Central Park
To hear, Cornbread Givens, Gilberto Gerena Valentín,
And President of the SCLC, Ralph Abernathy, speak
And to listen to the music of FD Kirkpatrick
That Everybody Has a Right to Live and We Were Marching
                                                    Down to Washington, DC,
And Jimmy Collier singing Burn Baby Burn – people jumping
                                                              out of their seats
Right on the Bandshell, there was a large banner that Columbia
                                                              strikers support
The Poor People's Campaign
The rally ended
The time was now to board the bus on our Long March to DC
We were 500 people from the New York Contingent
Many if not most of us were from the progressive movement
Along the way, we stopped to pick up, had dinner, rested
And had rallies in Newark, Trenton, Camden, Philadelphia, and
                                                              Wilmington, Delaware
Soon we arrived after nine long days with a thousand people of
                                                         the Northeastern Caravan
On the grounds of West Potomac Park on the National Mall
Soon as we were dropped off from the bus, we formed three-man
                                                                 teams

We were putting up A-frame houses every 15 minutes
With the permission and a ceremony of the Indian People
To have Resurrection City
We were a City of Hope where we each called each other
                                               brothers and sisters
It didn't matter where you came from
No landlord, no police brutality, no jails,
But it belonged to all of us
We were a secular city
Where we built a mural of the Hunger's Wall – Tell it Like it Is
                                                With our artwork
America, break down the wall – love is beautiful, hatred is ugly
– Love the Vietcong –
Cuba Libre – Viva Che – Freedom for Poor People (in Amharic) –
We the meek shall inherit the Earth when we stop being meek
Viva comunismo – Brother Mao
Love Malcolm and Martin
P'a la vida
Revolution or revolución
The Sisters of Watts for Human Dignity
We had a City Hall where the SCLC anointed Jesse Jackson
But our mayor was really Chief Big Snake by the people
We had our own zip code, the Coretta Scott King Day Care
                                                Center,
The Free General Store, and the Diggers' God's Eye Bakery
Free Bread Forever – Give Us This Day
A Freedom School, a Tent Food Center, a Health and Dental
                                                Center
And our own newspaper – True Unity News
No matter what your religion or philosophy, let us unite
Mano a mano in the spirit of Resurrection City
Since the beginning of our nine Caravans, we were under the
                                                mass surveillance
By state security
Denying our rights of assembly and free speech
And violence against us
Denying our civil liberties to protest our government
This was 1968 – LBJ, Ramsey Clark and J Edgar Hoover
The Dixiecrat and Republican Congress

We were marching for our life
That everybody has the right to live
For food, for housing, for health care, for Head Start, a living
                                wage, an end of police brutality,
An end to apartheid and break relations with South Africa,
Indian treaty rights, an end to the war in Vietnam, bilingual
                                            education,
When the climate of fear was waiting its moments to invade
                                        Resurrection City
On the early morning of June 23rd, with the Metropolitan Police,
                                            National Guard,
and tear gas, bulldozers, burning down our houses,
brutalizing the children, mothers, and senior citizens who were
                                            peaceful people
Over 300 people were arrested and sent to jail until late July
It gave me a real life understanding that the struggle is long
And the people united will never be defeated
Until a new world will rise with peace, love, freedom, and justice
                                                        for all.

## MARIA ESTRADA

## NOPALES

Don't eat with steel fork
Eat with fingers, timeless maíz
Patted out with each heartbeat
By your madre and abuelas
Your soul weaved in saliva
One trozo at a time
Don't drink Coke
Drink yerbabuena y café con leche
Café, ground in el metate
By your tíos and padrinos
Your tongue soaked in justice
One inhalation at a time
Don't dream of tomorrow
With gold monedas and dollars as your path
Dream of el ranchito y los Aztecas
Dream of running through dusty calles
Filled with loud aspirations
Your eyes looking forward,
Hacia better world
Don't cry tristeza
Over los fascistas y puta migra
When they come
Breaking through your front door
Like perros in heat
Tearing up the kitchen
Crushing your jarros with agua dulce
Using the bolillos to crack your teeth
Wrapping your tongue around your neck
In an ageless noose
Punching your eyes into a black blur
Wrenching your heart out with their laws–
As your children are
Ripped

Away
In a miscarriage of humanity
Don't cry tristeza
Over los fascistas y puta migra
You are the nopal dream
They fear so much
Let them tremble.

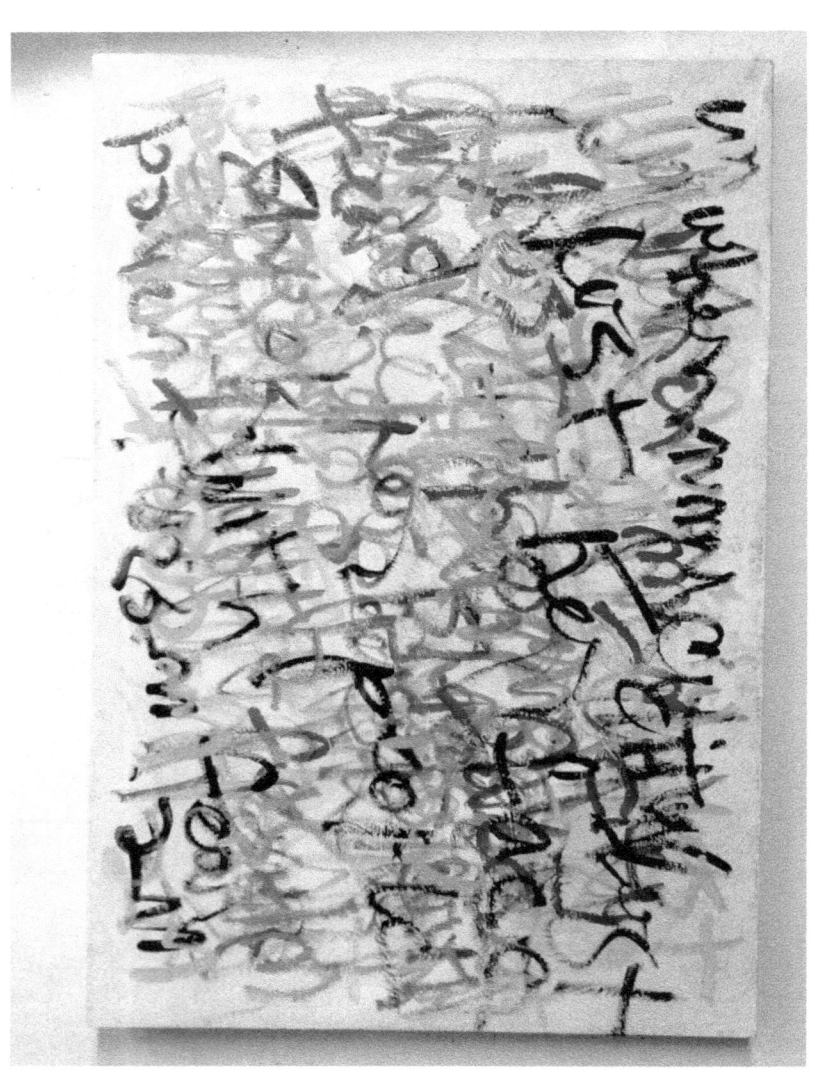

**PANDEMONIUM**
Victoria Brill

**AGNETA FALK**

**THE ONLY WEAPON**

> *In the dark times will there also be singing?*
> *Yes, there will also be singing. About the dark times.*
> *---Bertolt Brecht*

Such a gift to be born
that first breath
of a perfectly innocent being
without a scrap of hate

Just waiting to be nourished,
grow and reach for the light
one little heart, one little brain
eager to learn.

What a gift to be given
what opportunity to wipe
the slate clean of hatred
and racial bile, to cut

the umbilical cord to
the murderous past with
the only weapon worth
carrying: the love of other.

## MARCO FAZZINI (Italia)

### 13 (da CANTO DELL'ISOLA, 2020)

Tra barche nelle vigne parcheggiate,
case in affitto, e ritrovi per sub,
vane suonano adesso quelle storie:
una ricerca di miti che permane.
Mutati da vento, sole, pioggia e spine
le polveri dei morti stanno laggiù,
sotterrate, a fluire dentro al mare,
ad alzarsi con le nuvole di Kastelina,
Kampor, Sant'Eufemia.
Imploro perdono per aver taciuto,
per non aver ricordato dopo aver saputo,
per aver immerso il mio corpo nelle acque
d'un battesimo incompiuto,
mentre ancora spero
che il nemico sia finalmente
evaso da me quando la sera,
tornando dalla pesca,
con occhi assai provati
e nelle braccia stanco,
mai fu il vino così rosso
e il pane così bianco.

**MARCO FAZZINI (Italy)**

**13(from ISLAND CANTO, 2020)**

Among the boats parked in vineyards,
rented flats and scuba-diving clubs,
those stories now sound quaint:
an enduring search for myths.
Changed by wind, sun, rain and thorns,
the dust of the dead remains over there,
buried, then flows to the sea
and rises as clouds in Kastelina,
Kampor and Saint Euphemia.
I beg forgiveness for staying silent,
for saying nothing despite knowing,
for plunging my body into the water
of an unfinished baptism,
while still hoping
that the enemy would finally
be forced from me when,
returning from fishing at night-light,
with heavy eyes
and exhausted arms,
never was the wine so red
or bread so white.

*(Translated from Italian by*
*Douglas Reid Skinner)*

**MARCOS FREITAS (Brasil)**

**O ÚLTIMO JUMA** (a colher flores de capim-estrela)

a pandemia esboroou a tênue torre da esperança
famintos tritões engoliram o que restou de praia e selva
na entrelinha do dia ressoou lauta vaia ao ano
que ainda não terminou

muitos se foram, entre choros

a vida (sem saber) corroeu o tempo
deitou seus passos no chão
deitou manhãs em flores nos vasos

Amoim Aruká, o grande guerreiro,
o último homem do povo Juma
partiu para sua longa viagem
antecipada pela COVID-19.

Amoim Aruká, sobrevivente
do grande massacre no rio Assuã,
1964, bacia hidrográfica do rio Purus.
Comerciantes invadiram as terras dos Jumas,
atrás de sorva e castanhas.

Amoim Aruká agora silencia
e com ele a língua Tupi-Kagwahiva
Amoim Aruká e seu papagaio estampado em foto
de Odair Leal para o mundo dos brancos.

como previsto, de nada adiantou
o tal tratamento precoce
a base de azitromicina e ivermectina,
no Hospital Sentinela, Humaitá, Amazonas.

**MARCOS FREITAS (Brazil)**

**THE LAST JUMA** (harvesting white beak-rush flowers)

the pandemic shattered the tenuous tower of hope
hungry newts swallowed what was left of the beach and
                                                    jungle
between the lines of the day resounded abundant booing to
                                                    the year
that is not over yet

many are gone, among cries

life (unknowingly) eroded time
laid your steps on the floor
laid mornings in flowers in the pots

Amoim Aruká, the great warrior,
the last man of the Juma people
left for his long journey
anticipated by COVID-19.

Amoim Aruká, survivor
of the great massacre on the Assuã river,
in 1964, Purus River hydrographic basin.
Merchants invaded the lands of the Jumas,
behind rowanberries and chestnuts.

Amoim Aruká is now quiet
and with him the Tupi-Kagwahiva language
Amoim Aruká and his printed parrot in photo
from Odair Leal to the world of whites.

as predicted, it was useless
the so-called early treatment
based on azithromycin and ivermectin,
at the Sentinela Hospital, Humaitá, Amazonas.

os seus descendentes seguem resistindo
na agora Terra Indígena Juma
mesclados, porém, aos Uru-Eu-Wau-Wau.

Amoim Aruká, o grande guerreiro,
o último tatuado na face, o risco da boca, a orelha
em volta dos lábios
as duas metades: mutum / arara araraúna
o derradeiro guerreiro Juma.

his descendants continue to resist
in the now Juma Indigenous Land
mixed, however, with the Uru-Eu-Wau-Wau.

Amoim Aruká, the great warrior,
the last tattooed on the face, the risk of the mouth, the ear around the lips
the two halves: curassow / macaw araraúna
the ultimate Juma warrior.

*(Translated from Portuguese by the Author)*

# RAFAEL JESÚS GONZÁLEZ (USA/Mexico)

## TRABAJADOR(A)

El que trabaja con sus manos es obrero,
el que trabaja con sus manos y su cabeza
es artesano, el que trabaja con sus manos
y su cabeza y su corazón es artista,
así dijiste hermano Francisco.
¿Eras artista entonces, hermano,
reconstruyendo San Damián y la capilla
de Ntra. Sra. Reina de los Ángeles?
No conozco hombre o mujer que trabaje
sólo con las manos sin la cabeza
agobiada que sea o sin el corazón
pesado y doliente que esté.
Son la circunstancias injustas que separan
las manos de la cabeza y del corazón.
Obreros, artesanos, artistas
somos todos trabajadores —
nos ganamos el pan y ponemos
el pan, y el vino, en las mesas.
Si pobreza hay no es culpa nuestra;
es generosa la Tierra cuando no cae
en las manos de los avaros.
Si bautizo hay de agua y de sangre
también la hay del sudor.

## RAFAEL JESÚS GONZÁLEZ (USA/Mexico)

## WORKER

He who works with his hands is a laborer,
He who works with his hands & his head
is a craftsman, he who works with his hands
& his head and his heart is an artist,
   so you said, brother Francis.
Were you then an artist, brother,
rebuilding St. Damian & the chapel
of Our Lady Queen of the Angels?
I do not know man or woman who works
only with the hands without the head
weighed down though it be or without heart
though it be bitter & hurting.
It is unjust circumstances that separate
the hands from the head & the heart.
Laborers, crafts-folk, artists
we are all workers —
we earn our bread & put
bread, & wine, on the tables.
If poverty there be it is no fault of ours;
the Earth is generous when it does not fall
into the hands of the greedy.
If there is baptism of water & blood
so also there is of sweat.

      *(Translated from Spanish by the Author)*

## ART GOODTIMES

## WINTER OF OUR DISCONTENT

Expected snow
& its band of flakes
a no-show

No surprise
It's the dosey-doe
of cloudless skies

This drumbeat of tax cuts
border walls, coal scat
& plutonium futures

It's undanceable
Unsustainable
It's an off-key bully boast

Care frozen mid-step
Wisdom in flaming absence
Let's face it, we're furious

Realizing it's anger
that makes the floor shake
Calling us out to act on

our thwarted socialist values
Mad as shaggy manes busting up
through the White House lawn

Disgust pushing us
onto the Beltway dance floor
for a little Aztec two-step

A tarantella of protests is

the outside action that comes
from an inside movement

Outrage that will not stay put
Though, as one dead poet
put it, to give us hope:

In every good tango
there's a step backwards too
Nevertheless, McRedeye sez

no time for tip-toeing. This ain't
the ballet. Best be joining hands
Jumping into the mosh pit.

## ADAM GOTTLIEB

## WE THE PEOPLE

are remembering our name
waking up & taking what was always promised us
but never was intended to be ours

we the workers / we the renters
we the women / we the youth
we the houseless / the illegals
the unemployed / the disillusioned
we the Black Lives / we the Natives
the believers & the cynical
we the unsung / we the fire-keepers
the visions of our ancestors
& seeds of generations yet to come

repairing our wounds / shining our light
changing our face / demanding our rights

we the people who work double-shifts
we the people whose loved ones are jailed
we the people who are jailed for the sake of our loved ones
& deported & tortured / evicted & starved

we the people who built all this wealth
for men who said "We the People"
but meant only themselves

we the teachers / we the students
the troublemakers & the truants
we the squatters / we the dreamers
we the marchers / we the movement
we the rebels / we the rabble
we the damned & we the saved
from Atlanta to Seattle

come to claim the deal we made

we the nurses in the fire
we the maids & uber drivers
we who've always been essential
realizing our potential

We the People in Order to form
a more perfect Union in the eye of the storm
establish Justice in the land of slaughter
insure Domestic Tranquility from those who poison our water
provide for the Common Defense beyond wars
promote the General Welfare beyond prisons
& secure the Blessings of Liberty
to ourselves & our Posterity

do ordain this new Generation of the Free
& establish our Constitution

for these lands
from sea to sea.

## EGON GÜNTHER (Germany)

## WEISSER MORGEN
*(in gedenken an erich mühsam)*

zeitig wird der wahnsinn wach
streckt bebend seine glieder
draußen tost ganz wild der bach
übertönt der vögel lieder

nah steht der feind
hoch steigt die flut
die wache drängt
roh in die latrinen
fernab der freund
tief sinkt der mut
zum krieg bereit
sind nur maschinen

der weiße mord unterhöhlt
den mürben damm
der kaum noch hält die haßverzehrte meute
so manchem wird ums herz
nun kalt und klamm
er dünkt sich bereits des abschaums feste beute
unterm firnis der zivilisation bleckt
– vulgär und nackt –
das unrecht forsch die fresse
der trommler der nation heckt
unheilen takt
verleumdung speit enthemmt die presse

des gemordeten gruß aus dem grabe
er gilt nicht euch – den mördern
die ihr mit barbarischem gehabe
suchtet das recht zu fördern
das ihr befunden habt für recht:

**EGON GÜNTHER (Germany)**

**WHITE MORNING**
*(erich mühsam in memoriam)*

early on madness wakes from his dream
and shaking stretches his limbs
outside wildly rages the stream
drowning out the birds' singing

close-by stands the fiend
high rises the flood
the guard presses on
roughly into the latrines
far from any friend
depressed is his mood
prepared for war
are only the machines

the white murder undermines
the crumbling dam
that hardly holds in check the hateful pack
many a one in his heart
now feels cold & clammy
deeming himself already the scum's rich picking
just under the veneer of civilization
wrongfulness – vulgar & naked beast that be –
brashly baring his teeth & also showing his face
the drummer of the nation
conjuring baneful times to be
the press spitting slander across time & space

the murdered's regards from the grave
are not for you – the murderers
you who with barbarous affectation gave
more support to the law of might
that you ruled to be right:

die tradition von herr und knecht
mitsamt der willkür alter sonderrechte
keine gegner seid ihr die er achtet
nur verachtenswerte folterknechte
selbst wenn ihr überheblich trachtet
die welt euch untertan zu machen

er kann euch bloß im grab verlachen
und falls ihr sie gewinnt sogar
mit trug und macht und eisen
euer herrentraum wird niemals wahr
die zukunft mag's erweisen.

the tradition of master & slaves
withal the arbitrariness of ancient privilege
you are no adversaries earning his respect
all but despicable torturer knaves
even though arrogantly to subject
you strove the world to your tyranny

in his grave he can but scoff at you
and should you win the world even
with fraud & might & steel
your dream of the master race ne'er comes true
as will prove future's reel.

*(Translated from German by Jörg W. Rademacher)*

**BILL HATCH**

**PENNY STREET SKETCH OF THE SKIPPER**
*(for Lawrence Ferlinghetti, 1919-2021)*

From Nothing to Nothing,
Wearing an ironic grin and
A fine hat,
Back straight, naval officer,
The wheel at hand,
The compass within,
Forever approaching
That Beach,
June Sixth,
Nineteen forty-four,
A break in bad weather,
But not in artillery.
Back straight at the wheel,
Into battle,
There went a gent,
Always among us
But never quite of us,
Size drew him above us,
A floating fedora or Fisherman's cap and
An ironic grin,
Steering to battle
Against the
Same old
Same old
Nazis.

# MARTIN HICKEL

## FREEDOM IS SLAVERY

that all food -- cooked or not
brings only the flavor of more hunger
that each must starve before all
will act & that thesis & antithesis
collide & carve on a distant shore
the dangerous cliff called tomorrow
that the weak gruel ladled out
without relent -- again & again
never feeds you -- only leaves you
wanting more -- that you fear
meals might be lost rather than
risk what little you taste for
the promise of something better
that you dare not dream -- but
close your eyes -- imagination
untasted while your stomach
whispers be afraid -- be very afraid
life a dream denied -- a prison
sentence served in a lonesome cell
walls built of your own mind
that time before is somehow
different than time after -- that
now is not like then or closer
still to a beginning than the end
that time is not the same here or
there & all you know & waste
saying you are out of time -- for now
that it came in a box wrapped like a
gift & emptied slowly when young
quickly when old -- while in between
you wonder how long time will last
sometimes -- more -- others -- less
but always running one way only

infinity no matter for mere mortals
that you were told to study
learn history like a highway map
the past simply a road leading to you
your forward path -- a road more
sales pitch than route -- pictures
pretty ones at that -- selling goods
& services on profitable account
advertising sales more important
than facts -- just trust in the process
believe what you see -- learn the myths
pretend they are real -- fairy stories taught
many ways magically erasing suffering
as if winning without losing lifts an arc
out of the past all can ride for free
that time is a trap you escape -- go
on vacation -- play on the internet
swim to the bottom of a whisky bottle
watch tv & hide in a puff of smoke -- as if
time & earth are things you own but they
are not & without revolt -- your leaky boat
called ownership goes down without hope.

# JACK HIRSCHMAN

## THE RED CARNATION ARCANE

1.

If it could be done
in Portugal almost
50 years ago, the
Red Carnation can

stop the spread of
fascism everywhere
today, tomorrow so
let's get that huge

jail built for the 838
hate groups, Klans
and Nazis, Skins
and all those who

have to learn hate
is not free speech,
and we have to see
that they spend

time away from the
innocence of children
they despise, the
Blacks who they've

always terrorized, the
Jews they've always
lied about, the Gays
they've mocked. And

now the Red Carnations

have exposed the traitors
of the working-class, the
police, whose betrayal is

rooted and resonating to
those very klansmen and
nazis. But now enlightened
understanding has the cops

jailing klansmen and nazis
and beginning to deal with
neighborhoods as if they
were neighbors and didn't

wear hoods. And hopefully
they begin to think that
perhaps they'd had it all
wrong defending capitalists

and begin seeing Blacks
as their working-class
brothers and sisters and
children in a vivid family.

2.

Look at that! With
all the mongers of
fascist hate in the
jail where they

belong, just look at
that beat cop who's
admiring Beulah Mae
Dandridge's Garden

of Red Carnations in
the outer Mission.
Why she's even given
him her watering-can

and he's sprinkling the
carnations with water
from that sprinkler, on the
side of which is written:

American Ku Klux Klans,
American Nazis, you're
finished with murdering
Democracy at last!

## EVERETT HOAGLAND

## SELF-HEXED REX AMERIKKKA

> *"...they done fucked our mama and done run or shipped us children all over the goddamn place..."*
> *"...Down with the system!" – Neo-Griot Kalamu ya Salaam, re: post-Gulf flood disaster*

> *We've got to do something."*
> *"...a stable political organization...from the grassroots...*
> *....create a Left Caucus initiated by but not limiterd to the Black Left" – Amiri Baraka, October 2005*

> *"...It is essential that we always repeat:*
> *'we the people'..." – Sonia Sanchez, "Poem for July 4, 1994"*

who put the hoodoo hex on you rex amerikkka?
you founding father of sally hemings' slave children you
        who would drown all of us in the u.s. under
your man-made flood of bad blood you
who drowned many thousands gone in middle

passage...in cape fear river...in new orleans

you who drowned our ancestral african family
names in the holy water of those baptismals **We
The People** have a brassy bravura second-line to do in your
halliburton bottom-line you don't-give-a damn levee
saboteur you unnatural disaster of pox-infected

blankets tuskegee experiment "scientific" race-
isms benign neglect you who broke your own levee of lies
as you have all of your promises since the declaration
of your slavery-based "free" market nation **We**

**The People** have an upbeat dancing second-line
marching behind your mass murdering kind playing you

out of our minds escorting your dying self to the border of
hell while we knell you out with the red-white-&-black
blues
tune "liberty" with your own old cracked two-tongued bell
**We**

**The People** with history's bloodknots who you
call have-nots who indeed have never had any homeland
security under you are heralding in a new order **We The
People** having always been playing you when we cake
walked ragged

jazzed injustice high-five & slam
dunk our defiance of you from now to back when you were
an outright slaveship crew & right
up again to what we just went through in new orleans
which is hardly new behind your big easy behind

one of the capitols of capital (another being
the colonized mind) where you reign
over death for profit in the hood you who still steal
deal & otherwise sell souls having done it to us in the u.s.
since before we even got here the receded flood

of your bad blood reveals your graffiti walled order as the
open book of devilish lies it wholly is you commodifier of
c.a.r.e. & compassion you domestically violent white
sheeted terrorist

you who profits from polluting the planet sabatoging

all of earth you who are intent on the mass
murder or incarceration of all of us in the nation who do not
abide by your will

if you had your way but **We The People** peeped that & say
you had your day

rex amerikkka

you put a hex on yourself rex amerikkka
hey-day king of the may king of the gras
on a five hundred year old perennially new parade float of
                                          bloated corpses
but **We The People** shall reign ourselves
when every day is may day **We The People**
a high-stepping brassy second-line shall be

behind you & do
& not for a closer walk
with your t'is of thee economy
rex amerikkka but to usher you
and your warring "business of amerikkka is business" as
                 usual at all costs youth-killer-kind out
to herald ourselves in beyond white

2.

dove holiday card peace & sunday morning love
of one another
an organized coalition of us in the u.s.
shall drown you out with gospel shout righteous rap
dialectics in diverse dialects more than token spoken

word protest anthems movement mantras in unity &
                                                     struggle
to usher your deposed pimping
"show me something" ass out

rex amerikkka you founding motherfucker
you.

## BRUCE ISAACSON

## STANZAS FOR HEROES OF OUR TIME

At the hospital where Walt Whitman
tended and brought peach preserves
to fresh war wounded men,
they are dying again.
Doing it en masse, this time,
ventilators pounding out a ritual rhythm
to simulate the miracle of breath.

Nurse & doctor stand on each side, working.
Doctor, her hands move precise, careful, firm
o'er patient not conscious
but not without hope. Sometimes
it seems breath has been
knocked out of the nation.
But also there are heroes.
The helping professions who've long quietly stood guard
at the gates of despair, so many, so
unassuming: nurses, doctors, EMTs,
others who risk all
to establish some dominion for
benevolence. And courage—

let's not forget the courage
of workers who walk into contagion
with healing in mind.
What the nation most needs
they will offer, without fanfare
un-priced, un-ironic—under empty sky or God,
under whatever belief you may have—

they offer proof. Limitless & lasting,
practicing their craft
but not crafty, without scent of
guile or irony
they offer what most we need.
The kindness of strangers.

# WORK

The chores between cups of tea

What I do day in, day out

A paperchain treadmill

Keeping the masses' hands tied

**WORK**
**Yorkshire Collective**

**SUSU JEFFREY**

**A WEEK AFTER I CAN'T BREATHE**
*for George Floyd*

In the last gasp
of capitalism
contradictions confront each
other
   victims struggle for breath
   victor on suicide watch
the fires.

The president walks across
the park cleared
   by flash grenades and
gas
holding a brand
new Bible
for a photo op
with an armed bevy
of Secret Service and neckties.

Will we will wake up
put out the trash
pretend it's just another Tuesday?

## ZIBA KARBASSI (Iran)

**شعری از زیبا کرباسی**
**دیوان زیر برف**

امشب گردترین فرزادم
از زادم از دادم از دست های من بر نمی آید دست
در خبردار انگشت کهین و سبّابه از مشت
بین این همه اضلاع از پنج پنجاهه پنجه هزار ملیون
گردترین ماه یمانی این بوم
این بام و خاک و در
می لرزد دل
می لرزد لبان خشک
می لرزد سرب سینه ی فشنگ
می لرزد رنگ به چهره نداری
مادر و خواهر نداری
خانه برای وثیقه
دوست برای خالی کردن زیر پایت ماشه جیب آستین آستر
حتی کفن برای کفن و دفن در وطن که هیچ
حتی حتی نداری
تا نداری
نداری نداری نداری
دو چشم پنجره ی دلواپس
چلچراغ و اجاق گرم پشت همه ی پنجره ها می دانند
دلواپس ایوانی
دیوانی که زیر برف خوابید و دیوانه شد
سفره ای که زیر برف نشست تا خالی نماند
زنی که زیر برف موهایش را شانه زد
شعری که بی امان بارید برف رو سپید شد
تنهایی ی تاریک ناخن خشک
زخم باز زیر پیرهن جر خورده
تنها شاهد و والی ی عصر این میدان لنگی
که دنبال اسب دوید و
زیر گاری سبزی فروش ها گا رفت
بنگ
مرگ در شر شر عرقش غرق می شود از شرم این مرگ
اگر پا داشت در می رفت

## ZIBA KARBASSI (Iran)

## DIWAN UNDER SNOW

Tonight I'm the Kurdest Farzad
from my birth's give & take to my hands' un-razed heist
from the erection of two fingers, the pinkie & first of the
                                                                                   fist,
between all the angels of five & fifty & fifty thousand &
                                                                                  fifty million,
to the most Kurdish fourteenth night full moon
of flesh & blood    I'm holed out
the heart is shaking
dried lips are shaking
lead of the bullet's chest is shaking
the colour 'no' in your face is shaking
you have neither mother nor sister
nor a home to be bailed back into
not a friend to kick away your gallows stool
not a trigger in your pocket's ripped-out lining,
not even a shroud to be buried in, not a blood home,
no way   you even don't have an even
you don't even have your own shadow
you don't, no you don't, you don't
have
two-windowed worry-eyes
warmness of home-fires & chandeliers
behind every window, k knows
you're worried about the balcony,
the diwan that went sleeping beneath the snows & became
                                                                                           crazy
the table that sat down under the snow so as not to appear
                                                                                            bare
the woman who white-combed her hair under such snows
poetry poured so pure that the snow lost its white
the loneliness of black-cracked finger-nails
open wounds under ripped-open shirts

اگر آدم بود سر داشت به دار و درخت می کوبید
یا مثل شاعری غریب از باهو هایش بالالایکا می ساخت
و برهنه زیر برف می زد
بالالایکا بالالایکا لای لای لای لای کاکا لای لای
بالا لای لای
بالا لای لای کاکا

the sole witness of the limping revolver-butts
                                     *[roundabouts]*
that whiplash limbs on an old grocery cart
& end up under a bung of limp greens

Death would drown in its own shy sweats
this death if it had feet would flee
if it was human & had a head would bang its head on a tree
or like a stranger-poet from its forearm would fashion a
                                                   balalaika

and strum it naked under the snows

balalaika   balalaika   bailalaila lala-
    lailai  laila-lalai  la-lai  lie now
sleep now  my lai-lai
    my little one
       my bairn.

            *(Translated from Farsi by Stephen Watta*
                                *and the Author)*
This poem is dedicated to Arash Kaman gar and his four comrades who have been executed for freedom

## DAVID LERNER

### A PLACE TO SING.
*—for the poets*

there was a time
when I whipped myself towards glory

there was a time
when I required a stage so wide
I could
walk across it from ocean to ocean

a time when
time was a weapon in my hand

and I almost knew
that all clocks would someday
bow before
our beauty...

I'm still faithful
to this cry
though it grows fainter
as the years march through me...

but now that
time is not my club

perhaps now
as the room I live in
grows smaller and smaller
as the temperature climbs

I'm so hungry that sometimes
I eat myself

perhaps I can live for
a place to sing

a space for
my heart to beat in

even break
I'm rich in nerve

perhaps I can dwell in
a closet, a corner, a niche

maybe bang my drum
in the cracks of a street

in an alley
in a dark part of town
where only fools walk at night

for though
almost no one at all can see me

I can still see
almost everything at once

standing on
this bump in the road

so hungry for a turning in my chest
I'm ready to break it open
and do it with my hands

maybe this tiny cave
where we're pressed in
has air enough
to keep us going
today

maybe tomorrow too
if we're lucky and strong and wild

tonight perhaps I'll
learn to
live in the inches

tonight in some tiny joint where the drinks are cheap
I'll skin myself alive
and show what's beneath
to others as perfectly ruined as I

a place to sing

to shout
without losing our voice

or selling it to the shiniest bidder

the fine and tortured music
we trick from
the cracks in our sighs
and the holes in our eyes

is what we have
to crawl and climb to

as we spin in the wind
of this terrible age

a place to sing

my voice
still raw and golden.

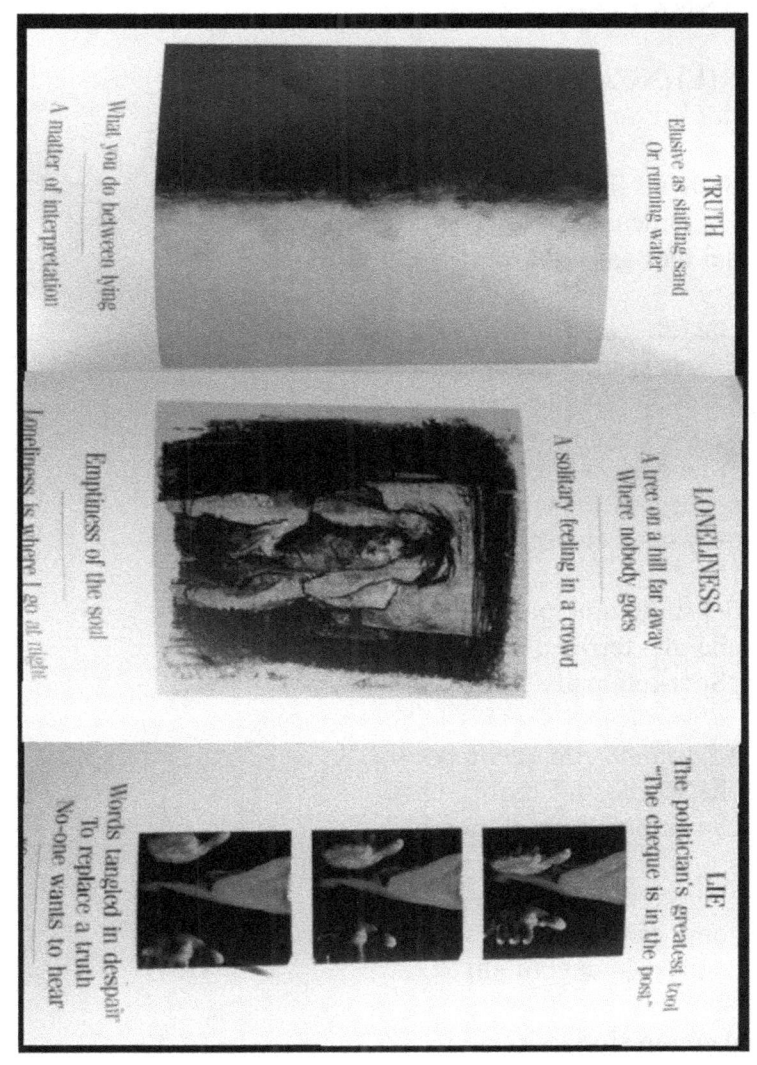

**IN BETWEEN TRUTH AND LIES**
**Yorkshire Collective**

## ANNA LOMBARDO (Italia)

### R(E)INCANTO
*(a Celeste dos cravos)*

Saranno fiori, saranno fionde
il r(e)incanto
dei tuoi garofani rossi!

Dal lato sinistro del cuore sporgeranno
festosi come allora
rovesciando quei battiti bastardi

A tendere la rete
che rigetti in mare
quei servi che servi sono

del sudiciume più sudicio
che mai terra ha generato
"Sparirete nella cenere della storia"

Vi diranno con quella poesia
che sconfessa l'indifferenza
che assolve tutto il mondo

Non verremo di notte, a gruppi
come cani randagi
o sull'orlo dei coltelli

Avremo fiori, avremo versi
e i tuoi Garofani Rossi
come eco che risuona

Nelle vene come fruscio
d'amore nelle frasche
sibilo di passione più che accesa

## ANNA LOMBARDO (Italy)

### R(E) ENCHANT
*(to Celeste dos cravos)*

They will be flowers, they will be slings
the r (e) enchantment
of your red carnations!

From the left side of the heart, they will protrude
festive as it was then
overturning those bastard beats

Stretching the net
to throw them into the sea
those servants that are servants

Of the dirtiest filth
land has never begotten
"All of you will disappear in the ashes of history"

They will tell you with those lines
which disavow the indifference
that absolves the whole world

We will not come at night, in groups
like stray dogs
or on the edge of knives

We will carry flowers, we will have verses
and your Red Carnations
as an echo that still resounds

In the veins like rustling
of love in the branches
hiss of passion more than ignited

Rapido brivido che s'imprime
come linfa su foglio scarno
come quel canto che freme

Nel petto delle madri
lungo le mattonelle
dei tuoi carceri a vita

delle prigioni sperimentali
del lavoro nero
del tuo fottuto lavoro nero


E saranno fiori, saranno fionde
Il r(e)incanto
Dei tuoi garofani rossi!

A quick thrill that imprints itself
like lifeblood on a thin sheet
a love song that quivers

In the chest of mothers
walking along the tiles of your
prisons for life

Those experimental prisons
of your black economy
your fucking black economy

And they will be flowers, they will be slings
The r (e) enchantment
Of your red carnations!

*(Translated from Italian by the Author)*

**KIRK LUMPKIN**

**HERE**

The names
of flamboyant notorious "leaders"
with their Trumped up self-importance
May be remembered long
after most of us
But, hold onto and nourish,
keep alive in our culture
all that leads by living example:
courageous love,
compassionate intelligence,
persistent caring,
gratitude for all beings
in the interrelated web of life,
So those that come after us
might inherit an inner compass
able to hold community together
as it guides them through
the perilous burning darkness ahead
back
to these places
we've called "home"
but have barely truly known
Where the final test of survival
will be learning to find
sustained sustenance
Here
within our local watersheds,
Here
with no place else to go,
Here
to survive
we will need to
re-indigenize.

# devorah major

## JANUARY 6th PROCLAMATIONS

"This is not who we are"
newspeak pundits splice
 in-between commercials
turning from the truth
that this is indeed
who
many of us are
american
seditionists and murders
racists and rioters and vandals
with a history of rampages
painted across the globe

ask a hungry haitian child
who she know americans to be
ask an iraqi widow
ask an afghani farmer
ask an agent orange deformed
vietnamese peasant
who we americans
truly are

take note
of the first people of this land slaughtered
the african people enslaved and tortured
chinese people sacrificed for railroad hegemony
japanese people imprisoned and reviled
muslim people scorned and exiled
the list is long and has no end

this government and we the people
with all our warts and wounds
this is who we are

I cannot point fingers at everyone
but let us be clear
the aberration is not them

so do we excise the cancer
or keep denying that it is part of our body
while it grows more virulent
metastasizing on all of our vital organs.

# ELIZABETH MARINO

## STEW FOR TWO VOICES

Every time is a little different
Dry red beans instead of black
tossed into the cold pot
mornings, at the first urge for
stew.
Add a cup of cold water.
Come back early afternoon
to little plump ones. Add
boxed organic vegetable stock.

Turn on pot. HI. Drizzle
a good olive oil
into your fry pan. Heat
Chop two fresh garlic cloves
a small white onion. Add
to the hot oil. Stir
till brown and fragrant
your best wooden spoon. Cube
your nice plump pork butt
steak.
Stir all till browned.

Season the pan or the pot?
It's up to you. Fold into pot.
One or two grinds:
fresh black pepper
sea salt to taste and
blood pressure.
A full dash of Adobo mix
an Urban Pilón lesson.
Grab the bell peppers!
Green! Red! Cube
a slice from each
Grab a fistful of green beans
trim. Add
Eyeball a small green
zucchini. Slice

Stir and let simmer
till beans are soft
then simmer LOW some more.

Our young people have
been dealing with trauma
for a long time.

You are aware of the chaos
currently affecting our city
on a regular basis.

Confronted with
Confronted with
Confronted with rioters

Black Lives Matter
is a hate group.

The use of deadly force
was entirely justified.

The officers were afraid
They could do nothing else.

"The Chicago Police
Department,
as part of, and empowered by,
the community, is committed
to protect the lives, property,
and rights of all people,
to maintain order, and to
enforce the law impartially."

A split-second decision
is very difficult.

The child's gun was empty.

## ANGEL L. MARTINEZ

## LUCY PARSONS OVERTURE

A song can only tell the story of one Lucy Parsons
Written in a suite of revolutionary movements
If one thousand rioters could not cause the fear of this warrior
Let our own struggle for freedom fearlessly rise!

How many hours have we fought so far
For an 8-hour day?
Workers in a class all their own, she knew
She knew no compromise
She knew acts of state terror at Haymarket
And every time she spoke out against this state of terror
Built on wage slavery
Her book has many missing pages
Yet I believe she'd rather we take action –
Not walk out, but take over!

She used her hands to defend life
From Haymarket to Scottsboro
As the unemployed march to this day
Hungry and poor,
Wipe this wicked system away!
We answer her call
against the bosses, never must we fear
And neither their guns.

## KAREN MELANDER-MAGOON

## REFASHION THE WORLD

We protest in the streets
Black lives matter
Immigrants matter
Homeless matter
In the prisons
Brown and black and white do battle
Who shall matter
Who shall shatter histories
Of misplaced hope
Scattered dreams
To piece together
Dream by dream
All colors of the rainbow
All life nourished on earth
That all may thrive
We protest violated lives
Unredressed grievances
Unmitigated loss
Unanswered sorrows
We pound the earth with anger
Yet she cannot help
The dreams we must refashion
Thread by thread
Rag by rag
Until we all together
Fashion a new world.

# SARAH MENEFEE

## CAKE

when people got tired
of shivering
in the raw spring

they moved

into the warmth
of the cake
we were promised

and so it begin'd

\*

little loaf cakes
with butter icing

he had three stacked
against his ragged chest

wending thru the line
appealing madly to
the blank-eyed shoppers

that one might
purchase them
for him?

'I'm hard of hearing'
said a hard-eyed
older man (white)

to the hungry
guy (Black)

here in the Trader Joe's
at Market and 4th

they appropriated
the cakes and escorted
him out

\*

do not let them
eat cake they can't
pay for

\*

I had written the part above
about entering the cake
the day before I
witnessed that

that that that that that.

## TUREEDA MIKELL

## IN

In…in
In …augur in….augur in ….augur
Inaugurate
In augur, in augur
In augur rate, rate, rate,
Rate nation, the prophesy
Rate the frequency the degree
Oh say did you see future
Inauguration
In augur, In augur, In augur
In augur ….rate nation
Prophesy
Fore see president
Swear, solemnly swear
Swear, solemnly swear
Swear, solemnly swear
Right hand up, left down on the
Buy bull
buy bull,
buy the bull, the bull
He solemnly swears on
The buy bull?
buy bull, buy bull
Swear, solemnly swear,
Swear, solemnly swear
Swear, solemnly swear
Swear in the president
set the precedent
Swear in the president
set the precedent
Swear, solemnly swear
Swear, solemnly
swear on the buy bull,

Buy bull, buy bull!!
Go bullish, go bully,
Manifest destiny nation-states
My way or The highway
In the name of …My country tis of ?..
With liberty and justice
For Just who?
Just ice for…
Swear, solemnly swear,
Swear, solemnly swear
Swear, solemnly swear
To protect and defend
Dress that poem up nice child
Don't hurt anybody
For the In augur, in augur
In augur rate, rate, rate,
Nation,
The prophesy
Oh say can you seeeeeee?
The Dawn came early didn't it?

Watch them swear, solemnly swear
Watch them swear, solemnly swear
Watch them swear, solemnly swear
Swear, solemnly and
How well did you sleep last night?

Huh? How well? How well?
Were you thinking, thinking, thinking,
about the inauguration
Inaugurating the nation
In.. augur… rating.. nation,
In.. augur… Nazi-nation,
A prophesy…of one nation
With liberty and just- ice for some
The 46th Inauguration in augur nation
In augur prophesy

Oh say can you seeee?
Did you seeeeee
The bully in the buy bull,
Swear, solemnly swear,
Go bullish for the buy bull
Swear solemnly swear on
Buy the bull, buy… bull!
Going bullish on America
Take back America?
Giving back America?
What you thinking, cousin?
Cousin, what you thinking?
Going bully… going bullish
Takin' back …takin' back
Giving back to the original owners?
Giving back to The Indians?
Right hand up,
Left down on the buy bull
Buy bull setting precedent
For presidents, precedent for president
For whom? Which hand
Swear! Pinky swear!
Swear! Pinky swear!
Swear on
Slaves, obey your masters with fear
Slaves, obey your masters with fear
With fear…with fear
Obey your master, swear
Obey your master, swear
Obey your master, swear
Your master
Your master
Obey your master…
And before I be a slave..
Swear, obey your master
Swear, obey your master
Swear

One nation under dog
One nation under god,
One nation under got damn!
Waz up!
That's my dog right dere
Right hand up …
Left down
Down boy
Down bitch
Good doggy!
Anybody get a dog for the president?
Don't forget to get a dog
to set the precedent for
Commander in chief?
Main temporary employee
Go between
Whisper Cuz an effect can become a cause
reinforcing the original cause producing same effect
with an Intensified form infinitum
Until inborn inbred reborn
244 yrs in, in, in
the in augur nation
Inauguration, inauguration
In augur's the pp code
Prophet predicate
God promise
Swearin' in the president
Settin' up Precedent 3
Swearin'in the president

Commander in chief?
Temporary employee
Swear
Pinky swear….
Swear pinky swear
Swear, swear em in on
The buy bull,

buy the bull
Go bullish
The highway or sideways
SWEAR, SWEAR SWEAR
SWEAR SWEAR
Swear, solemnly swear
Swear, solemnly
Enmity and hate will be placed
Between thee woman and thy seed
SWEAR, SWEAR SWEAR
SWEAR SWEAR
Take back America!
Take back America!
Go bullish!
Buy bull
Go bullish!
Buy bull, buy bull, buy bull
Swear…Slaves obey your masters
Swear …Slaves obey your masters
Take back America
Go bullish go bully
Buy bull
Go bullish
Buy bull
Buy the bull-shhhhhh

Don't buy what afflicts you!

# GAUL MITCHELL

## PHOTOGRAPHS OF AMERIKKKAN HISTORY 2B

Not a scrapbook for children.
Not photos for polite company.
These photos define Amerikkka

Woman running down the road naked, napalm attack in
                                                            Vietnam.

From a book called The Movement, Three men, one
woman, a group lynching.  White audience gathers, ready
for a a Sunday picnic. Young man poses for the camera,
his hands resting on the shoulders of his girlfriend.

Eye gouged, beaten, thrown into the Tallahatchie River, a
                                cotton gin fan around his neck,
Photo of a young boy, barely 14 in his open casket. His
                                mother dared to let Amerikkka
See what they had done to her boy, Emmet

Wounded Knee, My Lai, sow seeds of sorrow and regret.
Embracing those feelings do nothing for me. They've been
replaced with unspeakable rage. Still I speak them. We
have witnessed your blood lust Amerikkka

Amerikkka, you cannot sink your sins deep enough to
                              forget you are a blood thirsty nation.

We have seen your descendants, calloused souls, unfettered
by the deaths of others Children dying in forced detention
Mothers and Fathers whose babies have been stolen

We have been broken down and remade,
Cast not in your image Amerikkka but in our own,
and these are the photos that helped me see you as you are

## WARDELL MONTGOMERY, JR.

### SWEET BEAUTIFUL MONSTER
### (The Sexy Side of War: Satire/Exposé)

And now look at you, my sweet beautiful monster
I wanted you to stay home with your Mom and me and help
                                        raise your son
You could have gone to Jr. College and learned a good
                                        trade or business skill
That General said you would make a good soldier
They were looking for a few good men and women
The cultures of war love the sweet smelling sounds of sex,
                                        booze and drugs
The General said it was a "just" war for Democracy with a
                                        little collateral damage
He would personally recommend you to be the poster child
                                        for Uncle Sam
You have sex appeal; that Jenesaisquoi; you could not
                                        resist serving your country
It is the sweet scientific thing to do. Your Mom and I did
                                        not want you to go
For a long time we have been protesting bad wars for good
                                        reasons
We lost friends and relatives and you know how much we
                                        were hurt
We believe in blaming the country and not the soldiers for
                                        going to war
But we taught you the "Art of War" facts; you read the
                                articles, books and you saw the videos
To poke fun at us, you protested our protest with your big
                                        sign reading:
"WAR IS BEAUTIFUL; IT CREATES JOBS; IT
                     CONTROLS THE POPULATION"
You said there's a certain erotic beastly beautiful thing
                                        about war, rape,

Fires, torture, hangings, domestic violence and
                                        sadomasochism
It's better than belonging to a gang and doing drugs and
                              crime; don't ask, we won't tell
My kid said ugly is the new beauty and violence is the new
                                                      rich
Your Mom and I both agreed that you needed to get some
                                      counseling ASAP
The next day you saw the General and joined the Army
                            because you were bored and broke
It was all the wild drug sex life you expected and more than
                                      you bargained for
A sweet beautiful horrible experience and you loved every
                                          minute of it
Especially the friendly fire until they sent you home to the
                                          psyche ward
Laughing out of your head about what a great time you had
                            being a sex toy for Imperialism
After all like the straight talking General, you were just
                  following orders for the slapstick theatre of war
And my sweet beautiful monster, when your baby looks at
                                  you confused and crying
Because he does not even recognize his own mother (not
                                  like the before picture)
Martin was against the Viet Nam War and Malcolm said
                we were: "lied to, hoodwinked and bamboozled"
The General argued against the war privately but supported
                            it publicly; he follows orders
He also said he would take the fifth after drinking it first
                            and he was famous for saying:
"Never air the dirty linen of your war Fascist fantasies wet
                  dreams sadomasochistic menageatrois between
You, Uncle Sam and the Taliban that went insanely crazy
                   bad tossing you to the streets with the bottles
And cans you picked up to earn a buck to buy some booze
                    to share a drink in your free public housing

Home under the bridge where you are not even counted
              among the unemployed; it does not matter
Because war is so freaky, sexist and sexy. Don't ask, my
        savvy sugar horny honey bun, and we won't tell!"

## ALEJANDRO MURGUÍA

## INCANTATION FOR THE RESURRECTION OF DAWN IN HAITI

*Con tambor y maracca*
Ayiti—place of mountains
Arawak-Mandinga-Ibo-Dahomé
Spirit of Toussaint
Spirit of Jaques Romain
Spirit of Wailing Woman
Spirit of the People
Step forward in thunder & rumba

Spit out the demons—
Drum beat heart of mountain
Drum beat heart of river
Spit out the demons of poverty
Spit out that evil rot of debt &
Criminal banks that cannibalize
Your very children
Baraaph

*Cha-cha and drum:*
Ayiti place of mountains
O Creole Sondé miroir
Step forward Mistress Erzulie
Spread your wings like love
Step forward Ogun-Chango
Bring darkness to its knees,
Despair & madness
Will crash against your lightning bolt
Step forward Baron Samedi
Voudou the hell out of them bone suckers
Mount their vampire lairs
Their corporate boardrooms
Confuse their invasions at the crossroads

Let the zombies knaw
At their fingernails
And make them dance the dance of humanity

*Rattle:*
There is thunder. There is lightning.
Heralds of the new dawn
Where the Rada and the Petro work together
When workers earn a living wage
And farmer don't go hungry
And children have good schools with solid roofs
And hospitals are everywhere and they are free

Ayiti—place where mountains tremble
Where the sun squeezes through the gloom &
Dust of history
Beating heart of life
Beating heart of dawn
Hell yes dawn—sunrise, alba, sol, solazo

FIRE WATER EARTH SKY

Ayibobo! Ayibobo!
Ayiti—Place of Mountains
Ayibobo!

## MAJID NAFICY

## A FIGHT FOR KGO

You deserters of San Francisco Bay Area,
San Jose and Oakland!
you less than Adam and Eve!
You big mouths, little chimps!
How come you let go of KGO without a fight?
How come you did not fight for your dignity
And let a bunch of crooks and con artists
Wipe out your huge radio community
In the name of the invisible God of market
At the merger of two media companies?
How come you let go of that elegant soul
With a big body: Gene Burns
Who has the free spirit of a Libertarian
With the benevolence of a New Deal Democrat?
He can fight against mean-spirited profiteers
With reason and passion,
A good piece of salmon
And a glass of chardonnay.
How come you let go of that funny lawyer
With his R-less New York accent?
He can entertain and educate his listeners
With the colorful stories of his callers
And show how to compromise or fight
In the labyrinths of courts and law firms.
How come you let go of Len Tillem:
That icon of Northern California?
It takes you a Southern Californian
To show you how to fight,
It takes you a Persian,
An Iranian-American
To tell you how to stand.
Because I come from a line of fighters.
My first wife Ezzat Tabaian

Was executed in Evin Prison
On January 7, 1982
Because she stood for her dignity
And said NO to mullahs.
I come from a line of survivors
My brother Sa'id
Disappeared on the streets of Tehran
But his hope for freedom remained strong.
My ancestor was Nafis, son of Evaz
Who served Ulugh Beg, the grandson of Tamerlane
As a physician in Samarkand.
He taught The Book of Healing
Written by the Persian philosopher Avicenna
When the ancestor of greedy Cumulus
cleaned his dirty ass
With the palm of his right hand!
Yes, You have to fight, men, women!
And do not let go of your talk radio
Just because big money talks
And follows the law of market:
Supply and demand.
No! Money is not speech
And corporations are not people.
That radio community was more tangible
Than a gold mine turned into a ghost town
In the nineteenth century, California.
KGO was born in 1924
And became a voice of democracy in our state
And one of the best talk radios across the country.
It could create meaningful conversations
With interviews and listeners' participation
Without the demagoguery and bigotry of Rush Limbaugh.
I know it for a fact, first hand.
It was the symbol of independence for my American
                                                        girlfriend

When she divorced her husband
Who did not let her listen to KGO

More than twenty years ago.
She craved for an intimate companion
Who could carry a conversation
Intelligently and passionately
And she found it in KGO.
Even after we became intimate
She still called me Gene or Len.
While my girlfriend was driving between home and work
She would listen to KGO in the car,
And while cooking, dining, washing, gardening
Going to the bathroom or taking a shower
And making love at home
She would constantly listen to KGO
On her three separate sets of radio
Working simultaneously in her kitchen, garden and bedroom
Even when she was not home.
Sometimes she would dial KGO's number
and open her heart on the air
To tens of thousands of other listeners.
Sometimes she would go to KGO public gatherings
To meet Gene and Len in person
And participate in a public conversation.
Yes! I saw her beautiful trembling shoulders
When she called me one night couple of months ago.
she sobbed hysterically on the telephone
And told me that her KGO was gone
And its new owner, Cumulus Media
Had laid off Gene, Len and others
And changed the format of the radio
From a news/talk station into all news
Because the rating had been low
And the profit meager.
Yes! I saw her beautiful wet eyes
When she was sobbing into the phone
Telling that there was no one to stand forKGO
And she had lost her radio community,

Which was more important to her than her neighborhood.
One evening, my girlfriend and I
Went to a small vigil in front of KGO building
And held candles and listened to a speaker
Who asked us some simple questions:
"Will you occupy KGO's building?
Will you take part in a rally?
Will you write an article?
Will you talk on the air?"
You losers of San Francisco Bay Area,
San Jose and Oakland!
You lost your democracy to Cumulus
Which is an inheritor of a Californian crook
With the emblem of a rattlesnake
Who said: "I am not a crook."
You lost your goodwill to Cumulus
Which is a follower of a Californian con artist
With the emblem of a poison oak
Who began a war against the poor
By calling them "welfare queens."
No one stood up to him
Who gave welfare to big corporations
But denied it to the mentally ill.
I bore witness to it
When in May 1984
I moved to Venice Beach
And saw thousands of people homeless.
In the day that Cumulus took over KGO
Did you sleep overnight without a pill
And in the morning switch from KGO
To KSFO without an afterthought?
Shame on you!
You have no life instinct left in you.
You are totally useless.
Too much TV for you.
Too much booze for you.
Too much pot for you.

They have drained out the passion
That you need for a fight.
Yes! I am from the city of Isfahan
We don't fight by fists
We fight by words
and why not?
When a Polo shirt is $ 89
And a pair of Levis jeans $ 100
And an Adidas sneaker $ 79
And a cotton hat 30 bucks
Why should I get into altercation
And ruin my costly shirt or hat?
No! We fight with words.
This is my art from the city of Isfahan.
I will fight you word by word.
You go on the other side of the bay
I stay on this side.
Let us curse each other
At the top of our voices
Until the mermaids of San Francisco Bay
Hear and judge between us.
I am a man from the city of Isfahan
I know how to put words in a poem
Even if they are bitter as curses.
No matter what the editors of Poetry magazine say
Or the ideologues of the Cato Institute think.
I will transfer my anger into poetry.
Get up! Howl!
Let us fight for KGO!

## CARMEN NARANJO (Costa Rica)

## LA GUERRILLA (FRAGMENTO)

La guerrilla tiene perfiles
de plazas llenas en donde cabe alguien más
para decir en coro
hoy es un buen día y mañana será mejor:
las cárceles están vacías,
el hombre no es extranjero en la tierra,
ama y no teme,
lo aman y no le temen,
la explotación es palabra en diccionario
con exilios de practica y sistema,
un equilibrio natural,
se asienta en los rincones del canto
y se canta la paz de una guerrilla
insaciable en busca de lo bueno,
lo puro,
lo justo,
lo noble,
lo grato.
Una guerrilla que no acaba
porque es acción y no estado,
porque es agua y fluye,
porque es fervor y no credo,
porque es oración y no ídolo,
porque es palabra y es silencio,
porque es fe y busca,
porque es vaso y bálsamo
derramado, derramándose
en el siempre de la frente.

## CARMEN NARANJO (Costa Rica)

## MI GUERRILLA

The guerrilla has profiles
Of crowded plazas where there's always room for more
To say in chorus
today is a good day and tomorrow will be better:
The prisons are empty,
We are not
strangers on the earth,
We love and do not fear,
They love us and fear us not,
Exploitation is a word in the dictionary
With the exiles of experience and methods,
A natural equilibrium
Settles in the corners of song
And sings the peace of an insatiable
Guerrilla in search of the good
The pure
The just
The human
The noble
The grateful
A never-ending guerrilla
Because it's action and not being
Because it's water and it flows
Because it's fervor and not belief
Because it's prayer and not idolatry
Because it word and it's silence
Because it's faith and it seeks
Because it's vessel and balm
Spilling, spilling over
In the forever of the forefront.

*(Translated from Spanish by Barbara Paschke)*

**BILL NEVINS**

### ROSENBERG ANGEL POEM IN BLUE:
### A DEATH RESERVED (EROS AND DUST)
*for Abel and Robbie and Michael Meeropol*

*"It was the Red White and Blue marching down on the poor, blind mother justice on a pile of manure. Say your prayers and the pledge of allegiance every night and tomorrow you'll be feeling alright."—Richard Farina, "House Unamerican Blues Activity Dream"*

Sunday potluck at Albuquerque Peace and Justice Center
when a gray one asked who the FB Eyes here might be.
Robbie smiled, talked instead about children's playtime
glee-- his job, you see, the charity, and he's
that kind of guy, avuncular, bald, kind, bemused.

Was it really just all about scaring Jews? Did Hiss really
pumpkin- spy?
Did Venona shake you up? Why'd your uncle lie and let
your momma die?
Did you both cry? You seem so calm--Why?
Was it bad then? Like now?
How . . . did you . . . keep faith?
What do you believe? Were your folks naive? Did Joe
Stalin deceive?
Was it hard to be a famous son? Did you young guys ever
have any fun?

Rocking slowly on his heels, polite son of proper Ethel, he
waxed agnostic on the riddles,
dodged the well-meant gaffes, but rose gently to his bait:
"It's worse now, sure. They only took the Bill of Rights
away back then from communists
Subversives conspirators Blacks and "bad" Jews,

Yes in those days--Kookie days 77 Sunset Strip stop
combing your hair, man, and kiss me days--
Fulton J. Sheen starving hysterical naked days duck and
cover Lenny Bruce Le Roi Jones
Wright in Paris out of reach Mailer Naked and the Dead On
the Beach
Paul Robeson Old Man Moon River Just Keeps Rollin'
Along
House Unamerican J. Edgar's Tu Tu Blues Activity
Screams
In Pleasantville before the color washed in:
Giant ants in the sewers and Godzilla Rodan Body
Snatchers days,
Madeline Murray O Hare for God's Sake days
Yet Howdy Doody had Flub a Dub and Buffalo Bob to
hold him tight
and Batman had Robin and Sky King had his decoder ring
to save us all from Stalin's power
and some sharp stiff in a suit led three lives for all our own
safety but
still we worried yet Milton Berle funny "good" Jew and
other good ones walked free
and the USA saved them from evil doers, too
on tv Roy Cohn and that judge were good ones too, though
Jews--you never knew, did you?
Back then, of course, the country killed only traitor spies
and their wives who wouldn't talk
Father mother . . . THESE days they say all of us Jew or
not Black or not Arab or not Christian or not socialist or not
good or not talk or not--must give up Constitutional
niceties liberal vanities
for security--since the world changed, after all--
but, we'll be okay if we're good enough
conspiracy runs through every waking day and televison
dreams jar us awake 24
dirty bomb in L.A. psycho Saudis withboxcutters in our
showers

    don't sleep too sound you could wake up dead
   you're either with us or you're with them with terror

Terror! Juneteenth, Fifty-Three I was five and loved my
            Daddy who kept me safe and
who loved Joe McCarthy--Catholic and Irish, too--on our
                    boxy tv:
"He's against our enemies, Billy. He doesn't hold back."
"Patton should have pushed to Moscow and MacArthur
           should have bombed Peking."
Victory at Sea--Dad's pals burned up on carrier decks the
          smoke must have smelled so bad
  before Christmas in Hawaii" that day of infamy
and I saw his picture in his Navy suit with a big black eye
                    smiling
      he never pulled a punch my old man
so, Dad explained Chinese torture drip drip drip enemies all
              about nails pulled out
  like the Iroquois did to Jesuits or Korea War snow and
         blood snake pits Russian roulette
like Chris Walken-DeNiro later on too true too Hollywood
                     true
Jap death march Bataan lessons give them a bayonet in the
              gut like this, Bill
 he showed me the drill thrust, twist, kill--with a kitchen
           mop--so I grew up scared but
Robbie smiled that day at the good old P and J, all those
             long years now past
and I felt brave and safe, now at last as I once did in the
          Blessed Virgin's blue embrace.

"Meryl Streep overdid Mama's accent, still she was great"
         And Pacino nailed Cohn like Christ
In that too-public execution in Mel Gibson's blockbuster
              Passion of the Christ
Conspiracy and Passion was the charge against the
Rosenbergs--Not treason, Not giving Russia the Bomb

Two people passionately talking—Conspiracy in the eyes
of Roy Cohn and The Law!
They fried her for unflinching love (passion). And him for
discipline, loyalty, staying true
to his comrades, his beliefs, to his living love
As Wystan Auden advised "September Thirty Nine" when
the Big War loomed—
"Love one another or die"
Those tender comrades stood together in separate cells cold
time dripping
til that fast hot shock hit their heartsmoke rose from their
skulls
private faith in public view godless believers in what they
knew to be true in the long march of History Her Story His
Theirs and Ours
The good peoples' lawyer in his fedora held their sons' little
hands in the newspaper shots
protected the kids when he could –yet, the headlines
crowed:
"Your momma your poppa are dead!"
First time in America a family was wiped out"lawfully",
not just lynched
And in cold public view in cold blood too
Justice Douglas good man and true tried to stay their death
shocks but failed
supremely over ruled history happens and then you die.

Yet, of late, it is said Saddam Hussein that awful man nd
his horrid sons Did horrible things
as moms and dads watched their kids tormented as children
watched their chained parents writhe and could never touch
them again ever again
orphans--Jesus wept while his dad watched silent so they
say Abu Ghraib Gitmo--all those backwater swamps where
they drag the accused to the tree limbs of the gallant CSA
now risen again in USA--Strange Fruit, Billie sang—

Abe Meeropol good father, gave the boys his own name to
hide them from tv, press, killer eyes
after June 19, '53 and hewrote that song for Billie, y'know-
-he was a commie poet, too
and he wrote Old Blue Eyes Frankie's forgotten wartime
hit, "The House I Live In", which goes like this:
*What is America to me? The house I live in*
*The air feeling free The right to speak your mind out*
*The million lights I see. But especially the people*
*That's America to me.*

Their parents's life lights sparked out when the State
tripped the switch
but those boys did not die did not run grew to men
with sparks snapping in their hearts who conspire in the
empire conspire in love
in mad sane calm raging undying fire of mortal angels in
America
of course some nights still even they with us the less brave
might murmur dear old Wystan's lost Times Square prayer:
*"Defenseless under the night . . . Ironic points of light . . .*
*May I, composed like them*
*Of Eros and of dust, Beleaguered by the same Negation*
*and despair, Show an affirming flame."*

2006-2021

# CARLO PARCELLI

## BARRY THE BAPTIST READS ABOUT JULIAN ASSANGE IN THE GUARDIAN OVER A CAMDEN'S AT THE BLIND BEGGAR

What ya make a this bloke Assange
    Wastin' away in Belmarsh
For grassin' on them Yankee gangsters?
    What we blokes should be apin'
The Circus or – what the yanks call it –
    The Company, the CIA.
When they get caught thieven' and murderin'
    They put the constable away;
Throw truf in solitary
    Til it bounce off the walls.
 Not to be on that Aussie's end for
What bull Bellmarsh Billy right in the head
    Confuse his baton wif a pen?
      Or truf for a gun?
 Where Charlie Kray done time
    And Charlie Bronson too.
Lockdown 23 hours a day.
  Bloody hard to work up a frof
    'Bout what Ivan do
When the shits on the other bloke's shoe.
  I seen what them stateside mugs done;
Shootin' unarmed haji from whirlibirds
    Leavin' them to die
      Where they lie and
Takin' shots at a Samaritan
    Wif his kids in an SUV too,
Wee ones wif their little pony lunch boxes
    On their way ta school.
Last time that be under Bow Bells
    It be the bloody Bosch.
Them fuckin' Yankee weed wackers laughin';

  They be a brutish, inhman lot.
   It's in their blood, shaggin' their guns,
All petty pall about losing their slaves
   And huntin' the red man
  Like they's bison just for sport.
And the Aussie's too
  What slavish do what the yanks
   Tell 'em to
 Wif two centuries of target practice;
  A reich's worf of salvos
   Upon the Abos.
Aye, they learned from the best
  A nick off the ol' imperial block
What our lot once stretched
  East ta west, Pax Britannica,
The East India Company,
  All that rubbish,
Now ta die for a curry and a flat.

They set this bugger up for shaggin'
  A couple of Swedish birds.
 And of course money exchanged hands
  Ecuador's elite got their silver,
$5 billion in IMF loans ta steal.
   Ya set meat out in the clearing,
  The beasts will make it a meal.
Stockholm what gave the dynamite prize
  To the fuck in Washington
  What run out of bombs.
   Assange's trial as fixed as the dog races
   At Shelbourne Park,
No doubt his
 magistrate,
   Arbuthnot, told Baraitser
   Do the 'right' thing,
Or her husband, Lord James,
  And his goons at the foreign office

    Might do her family in.
     Not in so many words, mind ya.
But otherwise that pretty husband of hers
       Wif a taste for gambling and whores
    Can join Julian in Belmarsh.
Sound farfetched? Sound harsh?
  The yanks have their greatest torturer,
Their Torquemada, Gina Haspel,
      As head of the CIA.
Might as well have Satan hisself
      In the Empire's pay;
Or might wikileaks get audit
     Of the black accounts
And find at top of the ledger
  The Devil's name be announced.

Humblin' it be
   Watchin' them stone cold killers
     At the Albert or Langley
Murder thousands - women, children -
     And walk free;
Get medals and stipends
   Where I ta keep bread on me table
And butter in the larder
    Clip one or two,
And but thugs mind ya,
      Worse than apes in a zoo,
And I be nicked and beat
     And the screws
 Not ta shit me out
    For a decade or two.
And this bloke, Assange,
   Wif no blood on his hands
Locked in the can, tortured,
     Broken; but shed no tears
    Cause mind ya that's
    What the screws do,

   While Julian stares down the barrel
      Of 175 years.

No, our kind don't join the ranks.
   We got too much creed for that.
  Don't kill no mites for one thing,
Collateral or no;
   Not like your fuckin' G.I. Joe here
What goes rippin' apart bodies
  At funerals and wedding parties.
Fuck 'em. Fuck all them yanks.
     Fuck 'em ta hell
   And her Majesty's Forces too;
    What don't force us
   When a stretch in Belmarsh'll do.
No, we gangsters don't join the ranks
   To fight the fuckin' rich man's wars.
We fight our own
    What beef we be the source.
We fight our own
  Where there be a bit a honor left
For all honor of them fucks in power
     Be bereft.

## JERRY PENDERGAST

## OTHER FAVORITE THINGS

Trumpets and saxes their axes
Miles, Bird, Trane
de and re
constructing pop tunes and show tunes

Expanding tonal tempo and pitch
combinations, unlocking
imaginations

Taxes, that fund sidewalk
and water pipe repair
Walkways/bikeways, for safe crossing
and lake, river clean up.
Currents flowing
with pleasant notes

Communities, where all schools
have working instruments for everyone
in music and science labs.
Imagination, compatible
with memorization.

City Councils that vote
to pay public school trainers
not for mega stadiums
for private U's
and professional teams
that threaten to leave.

Where tents
are raised for events
or back yard play
not as long term homes.

Where girls/women
move freely
in fashion they choose

Where melanin
does not make one
"a suspicious person"
while driving, talking, walking…..

Where a long handled shovel
or hoe
strikes hard earth
Digs holes to be filled

The digger mentally measuring
the depth, width, spacing
for plants, baby trees, seeds
and no one calls the digger unskilled.

# GREGORY POND

## RECONSTRUCTION BLUES II

back in the day
after sambo became django
and we were legally no longer slaves
reconstruction was dangled
before us like a carrot
but we never managed to grab it
though it seemed to be inches away

after centuries of servitude
our men murdered, emasculated
our children sold, our women raped
in order to ensure our survival
we had to grin to bear the pain
before we labored through birth of a nation
feeling the pinch of derision and hate
years after burning crosses
repeated lynchings and klansman rage

sad to say we're still reconstructing
still recovering after restless decades
with hell much closer than heaven
while equality got lost in space
black woman and man
made some gains but
never better than second place
our lives continually marginalized
victims of an economic system
based on power, class and race

we're sick of singing kumbaya
we're tired of rhyming do-re-mi
waiting for some liberty bell to toll
to finally set us free

to save us from the choke of the rope
the pressure of the knee
from under the thumb
or the wrong end of a gun
in the hands of racist police

no more chants of "we shall overcome"
now we rant "no justice, no peace!"

**JEANNE POWELL**

## DID
## YOU KNOW?

[Fruitvale
BART station, Oakland CA,
January 1, 2009]

my country 'tis of thee
sweet land of liberty
of thee I sing

did you know before today
a bullet fired in disdain,
callous indifference
into a young father's back
as he lies face down on harsh cement
will power through, race through
his body prone
bounce off the pavement cold
and splash back into vital organs
like the heart and spirit and soul,
leaving no room for compromise,
explanation
or forgiveness
and no time to say goodbye
to his lovely baby daughter?

but you know now…

*Of thee I sing*

[for Oscar Grant]

**SLEEP**
**Alex Mildrovich**

# MIKE PUICAN

## DEMOCRACY HAS LIFTED ITS VOICE

*Democracy must be something more than two wolves
and a sheep voting on what to have for dinner. --
James Bovard*

Democracy has lifted its voice and boarded its windows.
Democracy has entered the room. "All rise."
Democracy is a bag of M&Ms with no blue ones.
Democracy stands outside your window singing sweet
songs of love.
Democracy has chops.
It dances at bars, has too many Manhattans, tells you it
loves you,
tails you through department stores,
and the iron gates of its asylums.
Democracy, your assembly halls are filled with tears.
Chamber of dicks.
Holy are the poor but let's table that for another meeting.
Democracy needs to defend itself against other
democracies—
Mexican democracies, Philippine democracies,
Beninian and Botswanaian democracies, not to mention
those pesky local democracies with stockpiles
of semi-automatic weapons and home-made baked goods.
Democracy is outside your door blowing the leaves off
your lawn.
So tell me . . . how do we settle this argument?

## JUAN HERNÁNDEZ RAMÍREZ (Mexico)

## MASEUALTLAMACHTIJKETL

Tlen nepa naui tlaketsalmej
tlen kalsosoli
iuan ika xochitlatsotsontli,
ejekatlajpaloli nijualika.

Nojaj tijpiaj kostik sintli
tlen kipajtok tlatlauak mestli
ipan konemej inxayak
tlen ta tijuika ipan tlajkuilolkuauitl.

Uajkapayotl tlali momaj
tlen ipan tlikuasejlotl motlapanki
inik tlatlauis tlatlayouatok pamitl
tlen axkanaj kikomej kitlauiliaj.

Maseualtlamachtijketl,
ajkia tojuantij ta tijmati.
Tiochiualkoyoli ta tijmati
iuan tlen kualmej iuan axkualmej ejekamej.

Xinechijli tlajmelauak motlajtol
iuan tlaj moteso auatl iuan tetl
inik sentika tlajlamikilis ipan akali
sentika uelis sejkanok tianejnemisej.

Se kuauitl nokuik
mijtotili uajkapatl
tlen se tlatsotsontli kiuikaj
tlen sekinok axiuikal,
ijkatsa uelis timotlajpalosej.

Maseualtlamachtijketl,
onkaj sitlalimej iuan totomej kuikatl

## JUAN HERNÁNDEZ RAMÍREZ (Mexico)

## INDIGENOUS TEACHER

From the four pitchforks
of the old house
and with flower music,
I bring the wind of greeting.

We still have the yellow corn
which has painted brown moons
on the children's faces
that you carry through the tree of letters.

Your hands are from the primal
mud that splintered into sparks
to illuminate the dark furrow
that fireflies do not light up.

Indigenous teacher,
you know who we are.
you know about the sacred *coyol*
and good and toxic winds.

Tell me if your word is true
and if you have roots of oak and stones
so that together in the boat of thought,
you and me, we can navigate in otherness.

My song is a tree
of ancestral dances
that carry a rhythm
oblivious to others,
but we can shake hands.

Indigenous teacher,
there are songs of birds and stars

tlen tlatlauiaj
ika totlauil.

In ueuejtlajtoli
tlatsotsontli, kiuauitl mijtotili,
xochipitsauak, pixkailjuitl
ika kopalij iuan tlaxcali inajuiyaka
san ika toxochitlajtoli uelis moijkuilos.

Ta, maseualtlamachtijketl,
tlen uelis tetsakuali kikualchijchiuas
tlen tiochiualkoatl
sintli toxayak tech makatok.

¿Kanij tiitstokej?
¿Ajkia tojuantij?
¿Kanij tiouij?
¿Tlen elis tokoneuaj?
¿Tlen intlajtol toueyitatauaj tijmakatokej tlen ipatij?
¿Tijmatij ajkia tojuantij inik tijmatisej kanji tiouij?

Tlamachtijketl nimits tlajpaloua
tlen ipan naui tlanextili,
ni mits kauilia iajuiyaka xolontok tlali
iuan iajuiyaka miauaxoxhitl.

that only ignite
with our light.

The word of the ancestors,
the music, the dance of the rain,
the xochipitsauak, the harvest ritual
with the scent of copal and the taste of tortilla,
they can only be written with our poems.

It is you, indigenous teacher,
who can rebuild the pyramid
of the sacred serpent
that has given us the face of corn.

Where are we?
Who are we?
Where are we going?
What will become of our children?
Have we given value to the word of the grandparents?
Do we know who we are in order to know where we are going?

I salute you teacher
from the four cardinal points,
I leave you the smell of wet earth
and the taste of the ear of corn.

*(Translated from Nahuatl by John Curl)*

## FERNANDO RENDÓN (Colombia)

## EL HOMBRE QUE LEE TRANQUILO

El hombre que lee tranquilo esta mañana
en las orillas del lago Hoan Kiem, en Hanoi, en tiempos de
paz,
sabe que bajo sus rizadas aguas duerme la espada de Le
Loi,
que hizo retroceder a los conquistadores en un tiempo
difícil para el país.
Lo sabe también el Templo de la Montaña de Jade.
La dulce anciana que me ofrece sonriendo a mi paso
una naranja amarilla como un pequeño sol,
sabe que los cham, los jemeres, los mongoles y los
japoneses ya se fueron,
y que los chinos que ocuparon sus tierras por mil años no
regresarán.
El hombre silencioso que habló esta noche
en la galería de arte de la capital, recuerda que un
guerrillero vietnamita
fue abatido por un tiro de pistola de un ocupante francés,
junto al muro de la casa de sus padres, en la aldea Chua,
donde los sembradores de arroz escriben poesía.
El pescador arrojó ayer su anzuelo al estanque en espera de
un pez,
preserva en su memoria aquel mediodía de abril
cuando Le Van Phuong derribó con su tanque
la puerta del Palacio de Saigón
mientras caían del cielo racimos de asesinos,
que intentaban huir en helicópteros.
Entonces los habitantes del norte y del sur,
separados por el enemigo,
pudieron cruzar el puente de Hien Lương
para abrazarse de nuevo y poner fin a su dolor.
De esta manera pudo reconstruirse el país.

## FERNANDO RENDÓN (Colombia)

## THE MAN WHO CALMLY READS

The man who calmly reads this morning
on the banks of Lake Hoan Kiem, in Hanoi, in peaceful
    times,
knows that beneath its wavy waters sleeps the sword of
    Le Loi,
who made the conquerers retreat during a difficult time
    for the country.
He also knows the Jade Mountain Temple.
The sweet old woman who, smiling as I walked by,
offered me a yellow orange like a little sun,
knows that the Cham, the Khmer, the Mongolians, and the
    Japanese are already gone,
and that the Chinese who occupied these lands for a
    thousand years
will not return.
The quiet man who spoke tonight
in the Capital's art gallery remembers that a Vietnamese
    soldier
was taken down by a gunshot from a French occupier
next to the wall of his parents' house, in the town of Chua,
where the rice farmers write poetry.
The fisherman yesterday cast his hook into the pond hoping
    for a fish,
he keeps the memory of that April midday
when Le Van Phuong with his tank demolished
the gate of the Presidential Palace of Saigon
while from the sky fell clusters of assassins,
who intended to flee in helicopters.
Then the residents of the north and the south,
separated by the enemy,
could cross the bridge of Hien Luong
to again embrace and put an end to their sorrow
In this way the country could rebuild itself.

La sangre derramada permanece en la memoria, pues ha
llegado al mundo para permanecer en él.
Sobre la piedra viva se erige la imagen de los siglos,
pero el mundo no aprende la lección,
Todavía no cree que puede terminar la pesadilla.
Querido mundo, escucha de nuevo al corazón alado.
Con siglos de horror se paga el nihilismo.
Un pueblo atraviesa los siglos para hablarte.
Su leyenda circula sin cesar las arterias del Gran Cuerpo.
Como el vivir, no se olvida nunca el lenguaje de los libres.
Respira mucho más hondo que la muerte.
Una nueva lengua reconquistará las posiciones perdidas.
La siembra de colores se restaura con la sangre del
                                  sacrificio de los pueblos.
Si el amor pudo reconstituir tantos desastres,
así mismo recobrará en su antiguo esplendor al universo.

The blood spilled remains in the memory,
and it has come to the world to remain here.
Atop the living stone the image of the centuries is raised,
but the world doesn't learn the lesson.
It still doesn't believe that it can end the nightmare.
Dear world, listen again to the soaring heart.
Nihilism pays the price with centuries of horror
People cross the centuries to speak to you.
Its tale endlessly circulates in the arteries of the Great Body
As it lives, it never forgets the words of the free
It breathes much more deeply than death
A new language will take back the lost locations
The planting of colors will be restored with the blood of
                                      the people's sacrifice.
If love can reconstruct so many disasters,
in the same way the universe can recover its ancient
splendor.

*(Translated from Spanish by Barbara Paschke)*

## LEW ROSENBAUM

## WHAT THE GHOSTS TELL US
*All that is solid melts into air –*
      *Karl Marx & Friedrich Engels*

Dinner at the Berek-Rosenbaum café.
Ghosts sitting at our table.
Diana stares through me
Brain fog settles between us
Hers or mine -- I can't determine with my caliper
She can't focus she tells me
No wonder I say
Grandchildren caught by the claws of
The dragonist court system
Children floundering at the ocean bottom of debt
And all around us fall friends of friends
All Breonnas and Georges and Adams
By other names
Ghosts sitting at our table
Wraiths of American fascist violence
The dispassionate dispatch of the bullet
Drives hot through the body unlike the cold
Steel of a Pythagorean theorem
The frozen stealy fingers scraping the bottom of my
                                                            pockets
Throttling any future of shelter and food
Tomorrow out on the street, digging in dumpsters

I'm shaking at the dinner table it is all very personal
I see all—my every one of my—grandchildren
Fleeing from police down Chicago back alleys
Blood pours from their wounds next to us keening
We sing praises to the millions
Taking the streets as if they were taking them back
From the forcemen of the apocalypse
Still the assault accelerates

But what else is there for us to do
If we don't fight for our right to survive
Confront the police terror, perceive how the cop's baton
Enforces the terror of hunger,
Of not having a roof over our heads
Of dying for lack of medicine
Terror inflicted on us by a corporate state
Unyielding in its murderosity, its profligate cavernous
Appetite for injustice

And so we sit with ghosts at the dinner table
Shaken every day. They nod skeletally at us,
They tell us we own the future, warn us
Drown terror in an embarrassment of red carnations,
Overwhelm starvation in a cornucopia of sweet mangoes.
They challenge us to seize this choice for our destiny:
Become fully human, end planetary fascist destruction.

**CASH**
**Alex Mildrovich**

# VINCENT ROMERO

## PARADE

the parade went down the road and played its songs to
                                      celebrate the wonderful
prosperous successful year the town had had and the sick
                                Native woman got ignored
as she wandered down the alley in the back

all the cheerleaders flashed their pearly white crest
                                    bleached and brushed teeth
and leaned in to gather blown kisses and wallow in their
                                    selfie youtube glory as
they too ignored the battered Native American man
                            staggering in the alley in the back

the richly adorned mayor and all the wealthiest honest
                                  trusty trussed up politicians
in their freshly washed waxed polished latest model
                                convertibles rolled past their white
picket fenced in america and they too thought it best to just
                                    ignore the starving Native
American Indigenous children huddled and sleeping in the
                                    alley in the back

after all it was the easiest thing to do this easy thing to not
                                  think of the correctly
politically named poor Native American Indigenous Indian
                              population as they ALL stumbled
in ALL the towns down all the ALL the alleys in ALL the
                                                backs.

## GABRIEL ROSENSTOCK (Ireland)

## BÁS SAGAIRT
*An Caitliceach nach réabhlóidí é,*
*múchta i bpeaca marfach atá sé.*
*An tAthair Camilo Torres Restrepo (1929 - 1966)*

Bhíos fós ar scil
nuair a d'fheallmharaigh
fórsaí an rialtais thú

Bhí 50 bliain ó tharla 1916 á cheiliúradh againn.
(mar dhea!)

Cén fáth nár fógraíodh do bhás ón bpuilpid
cén fáth nach raibh lá oifigiúil dobróin againn?

Bheinnse tar éis deora a shileadh i do dhiaidh
cinnte!
Bheinn tar éis tú a chaoineadh go géar goirt, a Athair
cén fáth nach ndúradh linn gur feallmharaíodh thú?

Nó an mbeinn tar éis a rá liom féin
nach scannalach an ní é go mbeadh sagart
ina throdaí Marxach -
ar leac na bpian atá sé siúd anois!

## GABRIEL ROSENSTOCK (Ireland)

## DEATH OF A PRIEST

> *A Catholic who is not a revolutionary*
> *is steeped in mortal sin.*
>       *Fr. Camilo Torres Restrepo (1929 - 1966)*

I was still at school
when government forces
assassinated you

We were celebrating the 50th anniversary of the 1916
Rising
(yeah, sure . . .)

Why was your death not announced from the pulpit
why was there not an official day of mourning?

I would have shed tears for you
be sure of it!
I would have wept bitterly for you, Father
why were we not told of your assassination?

Or would I have said to myself
what a scandal! A Marxist fighter - and he a priest . . .
roasting in hell he is surely.

*(Translated from Irish by the Author)*

## SANDRO SARDELLA (Italia)

## CAPRICCIO ANTIFA DISCANTO
*Perché non muore il fuoco*—-Pablo Neruda

1
ho fame di vento   siedo all'aperto
abbracciato al mio silenzio
ma può esserci vergogna nell'ascoltare
ma ci può essere vergogna nel tacere

non sento le corse e le risate
sento la rivolta sul viso
ai piedi del muro la bocca sa di terra
cammina nella luna la voce di Ma Rainey
in centotrenta chili di blues
scioglie la brina dalla mia testa

mi tolgo le ragnatele dalla mia faccia
nel velo opaco che avvolge la pianura
s'agitano strappi di luce   e
puoi chiedere dell'asfissia di George Floyd
puoi chiedere delle ali di Giuseppe Pinelli
puoi chiedere delle scarpe rosse di Luisa di Rosy
puoi chiedere del fuoco gettato nel campo rom
puoi chiedere dell'acqua del mare che ci accusa
puoi chiedere della lotta per la dignità del lavoro
puoi chiedere dell'io per sostenere il noi
puoi chiedere dei morti giornalieri per
                l'insolente affarismo padronale
puoi chiedere delle persone nella fame delle strade
puoi chiedere della paura dell'odio per lo straniero
puoi chiedere dei colpi che gonfiano il mio cuore

pietre   volti   maschere   numeri
baciami

**SANDRO SARDELLA (Italia)**

**ANTIFA WHIMSY DESCANT**
  *Because the fire does not die——Pablo Neruda*

1
hungry for the wind   I sit outdoors
clinging to my silence
but there might be shame in listening
but there might be shame in remaining silent

I don't hear the laugher and the races
I feel rebellion on my face
at the feet of the wall I taste dirt in my mouth
Ma Rainey's voice walks on the moon
in two hundred ninety pounds of blues
melting the frost from my head

I tear the cobwebs off my face
in the opaque veil enveloping the plains
scratches of light fidget   and
you might ask about George Floyd's asphyxiation
you might ask about Giuseppe Pinelli's wings
you might ask about Luisa and Rosy's red shoes
you might ask about the fire thrown onto Roma
                                      encampments
you might ask about the seawater accusing us
you might ask about the struggle for dignity in labor
you might ask about the Me that supports We
you might ask about those dying daily for
                the brazen profiteering of bosses
you might ask after people in the hunger of the streets
you might ask about the fear the hatred of foreigners
you might ask about these blows that pummel my heart

stones  faces  masks  numbers
kiss me

nel paese intossicato di ricchezza
papaveri rossi smarriti
ballano nelle mie mani

2
e io che nel sapore acre del sentire
mi lascio cullare dalla dub poetry di
Linton Kwesi Johnson dove pulsano
raggae e poesia  accompagnandomi in
un navigare a vista per
una rivolta al saccheggio dell'avvenire
           alla logica del profitto sempre
           all'abisso dell'ineguaglianza
           allo spettacolo dell'arroganza
           alla strage silenziosa delle api

nei bordi del cielo che sfumano
illuminati dal primo sole
io chiudo il pugno e alzo il medio

un gioioso rumore sfiora la storia
ai margini tra erbacce e pattume
è tutto un proliferare
           un ondeggiare di fiori viola
           di fiori gialli e bianchi e blu

cammino con lo sguardo di Spartaco
nei sotterranei della Storia

alzo il medio e chiudo il pugno.

in this country drunk on riches
lost red poppies
are dancing in my hands

2

and in the acrid taste of feeling I
let myself be cradled by the dub poetry of
Linton Kwesi Johnson where
reggae and poetry pulse  taking me on
a celestial navigation into
a revolt against the sacking of tomorrow
        the logic of profit always
        the abyss of inequality
        the spectacle of arrogance
        the silent genocide of bees

in the fading edges of the sky
illuminated by the first light
I clench my fist and raise my middle

a joyful noise brushes history
at the margins between weeds and garbage
it's all a burgeoning
    an undulating of purple flowers
    yellow white blue flowers

I walk with Spartacus' gaze
through the cellars of History

I raise my middle and clench my fist.

*(Translated from Italian by Lapo Guzzini)*

## LUIS FILIPE SARMENTO (Portugal)

## REFUGIA-TE

Refugia-te na tua consciência, sem cruzes nem crescentes,
sem arames nem muros, sem farpas nem ódios; e logo
                                     reconhecerás
entre as multidões de andarilhos que perpassam a tua memória
os teus ascendentes vindos de longe que te fizeram nascer aqui.
De onde vens? A que caverna original pertences? Que línguas
navegam nos mares e nos rios do teu sangue? Quantos deuses
adoraste, pedindo e esperando que o futuro não fosse este
                                     presente?
Onde estão as divinas respostas?
Refugia-te na tua consciência, sem o medo que os sacerdotes
do poder oculto te querem impor nem a angústia do sonho
                                     destruído.
Observa a renovação do mar, a regeneração do planeta
a cada ataque inconsciente dos loucos e logo verás
o poder das entranhas deste grandioso globo
como se fosse uma cabeça que pensa que a possibilidade
da derrota é a impossibilidade da vida e faz renascer
em todo o esplendor o mapa colorido do que na realidade somos:
refugia-te na tua consciência como anfitrião do futuro
e não temas os deuses, eles que são divinos que se entendam
longe desta terra, e abre as portas do teu humilde casebre
como se fosse um palácio contra a morte
e contra a babélica imagem do fim.

## LUIS FILIPE SARMENTO (Portugal)

## TAKE REFUGE

Take refuge in your conscience, without crosses or crescents,
without wires or walls, without barbs or hatreds; and you will
                                                soon recognize
among the crowds of wanderers that permeate your memory
your ancestors from afar who gave birth to you here.
Where do you come from? To which original cave do you
                                      belong? What languages
sail the seas and rivers of your blood? How many gods
did you worship, asking and hoping that the future would not be
                                                      this present?
Where are the divine answers?
Take refuge in your conscience, without the fear that priests
of hidden power want to impose on you nor the anguish of the
                                                    destroyed dream.
Observe the renewal of the sea, the regeneration of the planet,
every unconscious attack of the madman, and you will soon see
the power of the bowels of this magnificent globe,
as if it were a head that thinks the possibility
of defeat is the impossibility of life and makes it reborn
in all its splendor, the colorful map of what we really are:
take refuge in your conscience as host of the future
and do not fear the gods, who are divine and who understand
                                                            each other
far from this Earth, and open the doors of your humble hovel
as if it were a palace against death
and against the chaotic image of the end.

*(Translated from Portuguese*
*by Scott Edward Anderson)*

**BLIND**
Alex Mildrovich

## KIM SHUCK

## SONG OF EXTREME WINTER
## AND THE MINIMUM WAGE

*No one who works a 40 hour week should live in poverty.*
– Various
*Only the strong will survive and the weak will (perish)*
— Tim Boyd, former mayor of Colorado City, Texas
as his town went into another day in blackout during
freezing weather.

The relics of Spencer and Malthus rattle and echo
Music of disaster in a cold February
And in D.C. they measure the value of lives by the wealth they can bring
To someone else
Establish an acceptable rubric of suffering
A strategy to measure worthiness
In plain language we are each a mine
The mineral rights belong to someone else
Dry bones rattling as a poet and her brother do without food
Without heat
Without water
In an apartment in Texas
While in D.C. they argue acceptable deprivation
In Dallas they argue degrees of cold
On the news they argue about blame
The companies we pay for electricity owe us nothing
The elected officials owe us nothing
Our value is measured by what can still be taken
The value of a poet
Debated to the rhythm of Victorian bones
Rattling in a shell of community
A curio in the home of one of the super rich
Empathy another resource that has run out

ΝΤΙΝΟΣ ΣΙΩΤΗΣ
DINOS SIOTIS (Greece)

## ΚΡΑΤΙΚΗ ΤΡΟΜΟΚΡΑΤΙΑ

Έμαθα να παρατηρώ
τους καλούμενους «εχθρούς του λαού»
να γίνονται τατουάζ στο σώμα του κράτους

Έμαθα να βλέπω
αστυνομικούς να κάνουν συλλήψεις
με βάση φήμες απ' το Κατεστημένο

Έμαθα να προσέχω
νεαρές μαύρες και νεαρούς μαύρους
να πυροβολούνται χωρίς κανένα λόγο

Συνάντησα λευκούς ρατσιστές να επιτίθενται
στην naturaleza muerta της εργατικής τάξης
μόνο και μόνο επειδή δεν τους άρεσε η νεκρή φύση

Έχω δει αντιφασίστες
να οδηγούνται σε άσυλα επειδή άκουγαν
πυροβόλα και κραυγές στα όνειρά τους

Έμαθα να μην ξέρω
αν πηγαίνω ή αν έρχομαι

Αυτό που θέλω να πω είναι πως
ένα τούβλο στο παρμπρίζ δεν αρκεί,
ας φτάσει ως τον ουρανό η κόκκινη σημαία.

## ΝΤΙΝΟΣ ΣΙΩΤΗΣ
## DINOS SIOTIS (Greece)

## STATE TERRORISM

I have taken to watching
the so called "enemies of the people"
become tattoos on the body of the state

I have taken to seeing
arrests by policemen
acting on rumors by the Establishment

I have taken to noticing
young black men and women
being shot for unknown reasons

I met white supremacists
attacking working class naturaleza muerta
just because they don't like still-life

I have seen antifascists taken to asylums
because they keep hearing machine guns
and shouts in their dreams

I have taken not knowing
if I am coming or going

What I want to say is
a brick in the windshield won't do it,
let the red flag go up in the sky

*(Translated from Greek by the Author)*

**SANDRO SPINAZZI (Italia)**

**INCENDIARIA**
*(a Pasolini)*

Non si tratta
di parole
infilate a forza
in cruciverba
da terza pagina
di discorsi da convegno
tre giorni di dibattito
con cena finale
a carico pubblico
di bandiere
derubate del vento
dalla meteorologia
di regime
non è neo neorealismo
da cineforum domenicale
pellicola in bianco e nero
costretta al colore
dalla modernità
della vendita
qui si parla
di cose antiche
del prima vero
di un adesso fasullo
di mani impacciate
rovinate dagli anni
di rughe come trincee
attorno a occhi
che ancora vedono
un passato ancora qui
in un presente
che non c'è
di gobbe sulla schiena

**SANDRO SPINAZZI (Italy)**

**INCENDIARY**
*(for Pasolini)*

We're not talking
words
shoved
into a crossword puzzle
on page three
conference speeches
three-day debates
with a final dinner
on the taxpayer's dime
flags
robbed of their wind
by the regime's
meteorology
this isn't neo neorealism
at the Sunday cineforum
black and white film
forced into color
by the modernity
of trade
we're talking
ancient things
of the true before
and a fake now
clumsy hands
ruined by the years
wrinkles like trenches
around eyes
that still see
a past still here
within a present
that isn't
humps on the back

e pantaloni lisi
con borse alle ginocchia
e tasche rivoltate
di sorrisi forzati
prima della foto
e risate vere
nella festa del ricordo
pagnotte condivise
e fiaschi
e poco altro
in equilibri precari
impalcature alte
come le case degli altri
pause sottratte
a fatiche inumane
ora come allora
ma lo scempio
di sempre
si farà un giorno
combustibile
proprio adesso
lontano
un bambino grida
i panni stesi
sono stendardi
a una brezza nuova
non c'è più legna
da ardere
raccogliamo ogni arbusto
ne faremo una pila
alta
un solo fiammifero
basterà
un giorno
a bruciare
tutto.

and threadbare pants
with bags under knees
and pockets inside out
strained smiles
before the photo
and genuine laughs
at the Festival of Remembrance
shared loaves of bread
and flasks of wine
and not much else
in precarious equilibriums
high scaffoldings
like other people's houses
pauses subtracted
from inhuman labors
now as then
but the everyday
slaughter
will someday become
fuel
even now
far away
a child cries
the hanging clothes
are banners
for a new zephyr
there is no more firewood
let's gather every shrub
we'll pile them up
high
a single match
will suffice
someday
to burn
everything.

*(Translated from Italian by Lapo Guzzini)*

## DOREEN STOCK

## FOR JUDY IN MANHATTAN

> *But how alien, alas, are the streets of the city of grief;*
> *where in the false silence formed in continual uproar,*
> *the figure cast from the mold of Emptiness stoutly swaggers*
>     *——Rilke, The Tenth Elegy, translated by Stephen Mitchell*

A girl named J washing the floors of her apartment in
                                           Manhattan
vacuuming the carpets, dusting the shelves surrounded by
                                           canvases
of color said to me, "He's an alien. That's why/He doesn't
                                 get sick and die,"
not realizing it rhymed, as when reading Sonnets to
                                 Orpheus so busy
with the English I forget to glance across at the German…


J, watching the virus multiply by subtraction down there in
                                         the streets
Central Park now too crowded for those early morning
                                         walks of hers
until her last one, past the large tents set up in waiting. J
                                         now walking
the verticals, up and down instead of out and out, up and
                                     down the stairwells
pausing now and again for breath, her shadow bent over the
                                         next step,
the next…


A girl named J washing the floors of her apartment in
                                         Manhattan
vacuuming the carpets, dusting the shelves surrounded by
                                         canvases

of color thinking, "But how alien, alas, are the streets of the
                                       city of grief;"
not knowing it rhymed with thief, with chief, with fief, or
                                       maybe she did
as she walked the verticals, step-by-step-by step, and the
                                       bodies piled


high into the freezer trucks; and the mass grave trenches
                                       were dug
by prisoners freed from the local penitentiary to do this,
                                       and the bodies
unclaimed were sunk in, as the girl named J washed the
                                       floors of her
apartment in Manhattan, vacuumed the carpets, dusted the
                                       shelves surrounded
by canvases of color as that figure, cast from the mold of
                                       Emptiness stoutly
swaggered…

## MATTHEW TALEBI

## ARE THESE BEATEN SEALS ON THE BEACH?

Driving on Y street
like a French chevalier
the proud urban modernist
cannot believe what his
two eyes see.
The sky is gray, the air haunting.
On the sidewalk next to a tall boxy building
with a verdant, granite exterior
and a warm, bright interior
—a resting place vacant by night—
are aliens of all sorts, fellow humans
who've lost jobs or their sweet homes,
living in shelters made of nothing;
newspaper bedding is their belonging,
ridiculed as a cozy place in hell
or an illusive paradise
which they are compelled to accept.
Ignored-neglected
damned-and-rejected
beaten, thrown-to-the-margins,
half-dead, abandoned-by-life
stripped-of-justice, dear-lives-wasted.
Reminiscent of seals on a sandy beach,
corpses in the battle of Stalingrad.

Matthew, upon whom or what shall
the shame and blame rest?

# RAYMOND NAT TURNER

## BLACK LIVES MATTER...

B-B-B-Black Lives M-M-M-Matter...
Unless you listening to loud music;
shoveling snow; Or own a phone or car...
B-B-B-Black Lives M-M-M-Matter...
Unless you breaking up a fight; or your
brake light's broken...
B-B-B-Black Lives M-M-M-Matter...
Unless you a Chicago child unschooled
in Mississippi apartheid; Unless you a
Man not laughing at un-funny stuff and
looking up from mud into steely blue-
grey eyes; or resisting rapists coming
for your momma, sister, daughter, wife...
B-B-B-Black Lives M-M-M-Matter...
Unless you smoking a cigarette or making
A turn; Unless you a child scoring sugary
Snacks in the Sunshine State; Unless you
unhoused and have healthy reactions to
homelessness and its insanity...any city...
B-B-B-Black Lives M-M-M-Matter...
Unless you a doctor describing decent care
to a Mengele medicine man...from your ICU
bed...
B-B-B-Black Lives M-M-M-Matter...
Unless you caught trying to breathe...
between swastika of knee-
o-teen and long white arm of the law...

## DAVID VOLPENDESTA

## FORBIDDEN PSALM FOR DEAD POETS
*to the living word*

Keep a light shining in the darkness
for those who can really see.
Q.R. Hand, Al Young, Alfonso Texidor
and Lawrence Ferlinghetti all of whom
have just passed to the other side
of existence about a month ago.

Did this many poets die
during the Spanish Civil War?
There's a mysterious text
in the annals of that Civil War,
but there is a subtext as well.

The earth opens its hand to them
and the wind tells you to beware;
touch the water with its blue, radiant robe
and hear the peaceful explosion
inside of your body.

The four poets who have been mentioned
are invisible as they climb the mountain
whose pinnacle they will see;
don't weep for these friends,
weep instead for liberty
because Fascists are tearing up the alphabet
and these four aren't here to defend it.

Words are turning to ashes
as flesh is sliding from the bone
but the souls of four poets
are everywhere in their home
of radiant light……..

Listen for them, they'll know
when evil is ready to strike;
they know the battle isn't over
that's why they carry forward
guerrilla warfare against
the growling Fascists.

These four poets
are at your side
ready to serve you
and remove the hand cuffs
so they can help you be free!

## CATHLEEN WILLIAMS

## DIFFERENT THIS TIME
*For Ernst Thaelman*

*desire for freedom from racial capitalism*
*sweeps through us now like a wind*
*gonna be different this time – Nina sing –*
*another spring*

whole tenements burned in working class districts
roughly clothed defiant millions
crowded into city squares Hamburg
resist

make no mistake they were Communists
German Communists
who each bore death's scythe
stiff as wheat

1933 – that early –
first total sudden cut
across the throat of class revolt
Dachau

*so today on this matted ground*
*matted with blood and lies*
*wind rising young wheat dense*
*full of desire.*

# NELLIE WONG

## INTERIORITY, HEY?

Interiority, pungent and prickly, wafts from the pot,
Stainless and gleaming.
Brown rice kernels toast, relaxed,
in mellifluous heat.
My legs entwine the kitchen barstool
wrapping me in a haze of aluminum foil
while sunlight pours through speck-splashed window.
Soon Dubu Jijae bubbles in Gochujang. Red. Fiery.
I feel audacious, adding meatless
sausage balls, putting aside
scallions reserving spring
for evening's repast.

COVID-19 crisis inserts itself, irresistible,
non-discriminating and worldly when,
when a Chinese woman on a train coughs
and a white woman shouts "Oh, my god!"
Shielding herself with her trench coat, sinking
further into the plastic-coated seat on the train
while other pairs of eyes shoot
arrows of fear, panic.
Whole bodies move, shrink en masse.

Yellow woman pariah, again and again.
The exteriority of suspicion, "Yellow Alert" splashes
across headlines, modern-day "Yellow
Peril" springs into consciousness, the president
tweeting "a foreign virus,"
What "model minority?" What passivity? What dragon
                                                                     lady?
The blah of stereotypes. Ah, the orient. Ah, the occident.
Steal their labor and run. What invisibility? What lies?
Yellow women excluded before onslaught

of Chinese Exclusion Act
Yellow men killed at Rock Springs, murdered
in Hawaii, not real and buff and masculine enough
to grace the silver screen.
Just real enough to mine for gold, build railroads, grow
wine grapes, live in cramped quarters, fight the Cubic Air
                                                                                   law,
the right to attend public schools.

Chalk it up to ignorance wholesale? No, no.
Why COVID-19 is named
referring to its
eruption in Wuhan, China. There they go
giving identity,
racial and ethnic,
to a virus, dressing it with epicanthic folds, dividing
us, shelling us, tucking us into drawers, locking us
in prisons with psychological bars.

O we work hard, we do.
Bodies and minds in deliverance
of materiality of masks, hazmat suits, lockdowns
and pangolins hunted for their meat and shells,
bats for their medicinal use, their stewing, symbols
of good luck.
"Go back to China, bitch!"
"You don't belong here."
But I was born here.

## ANDRENA ZAWINSKY

### FEMICIDE
> *on International Day of the Elimination
> of Violence Against Women*

They marched in Chile,
red hands painted across their mouths.
They covered their mouths
with purple hands in Argentina.

They dressed in black in Uruguay,
raised signs bearing murdered women's names.
They placed red shoes on the ground
for all the victims in Belgium.

They hung stuffed animals in Honduras
from clotheslines memorializing the dead.
They laid under sheets in Panama,
toes tagged: soy tu novia, soy tu mama.

They marched carrying crosses in Spain
for women killed by men who loved them.
They clashed in Turkey with riot police,
their boots and batons.

They wrote 138 on open palms in France
for the number killed by beloveds this year.
They lit up the Palazzo Madama in Italy
in a blaze of red lights.

They chanted across the globe:
freedom, peace, justice.

# BIOGRAPHICAL NOTES

Known as the father of Nano poetics, **Razu Alauddin** was born on 6 May 1965 in Shariatpur, Bangladesh. He has translated selected poems of Georg Trakl, C P Cavafy and Ted Hughes into Bengali. **Amparo Casasbellas Alconada**, was born in Buenos Aires in 1983. Your Excellency, Free Will, translations of her debut collection of poetry, is to be released by SADE in Argentina. **Indran Amirthanayagam** has published 19 poetry books. In music, he recorded Rankont Dout. He edits The Beltway Poetry Quarterly and directs The Poetry Channel on Youtube https://youtube.com/user/indranam. **Adrian Arias**, is a poet, visualartist, and activist. In Pandemic 2020-2021, Adrian was commissioned to create a series of pieces related to both BLM movement and his personal vision of freedom, like BLM on the pavement of the Petaluma Regional Library, the altar dedicated to George Floyd in Somarts. **Ayo Ayoola-Amale** is acknowledged as a poet for positive social change. Her poems are concerned with confronting the problem of violence, racism and the breakdown of human community. She has been a guest poet at national, and international poetry festivals and literary events. **Mahnaz Badihian** is a poet, painter, and translator. She edited an international anthology of Covid-19 poetry and art published in 2020. Currently, she's working on the novel Gohar. Her painting is the back cover of this anthology. **Lisbit Bailey** is a member of the Revolutionary Poets Brigade of San Francisco and the Archivist for the San Francisco Maritime National Historical Park.She is one of the three editors of this Anthology. **Lynne Barnes** is the author of the poetic memoir, Falling into Flowers (2017), a finalist for the 2018 Eric Hoffer Book Award. Her work appears in Poets 11Fog and Light: San Francisco through the Eyes of the Poets who Live Here and Light on the Walls of Life—a tribute anthology to Lawrence Ferlinghetti. **Virginia Barrett** is a poet, artist, and educator. Her six books of poetry include Between Looking (2019, Finishing Line Press) and Crossing Haight—San Francisco poems (2018, Jambu Press). She has taught poetry and visual art throughout the San Francisco Bay Area. **Bengt Berg** is a Swedish poet and activist who's published 40 books, mostly of poetry, which have been translated into many languages. He was a member of the Swedish Parliament from 2010-2014 representing the Left Party. **Lincoln Bergman** is a poet, editor, and educator who served as Poet Laureate of Richmond CA. He's a member of the Revolutionary Poets Brigade, a co-founder of the Freedom Archives, and author of Chants of a Lifetime, a collection of his poetry. **Judith Ayn Bernhard** is the author of a poetry collection, Prisoners of Culture, and a book of short stories, Marriages. She is an editor of Andover Street Archives Press. **Scott Bird** is a poet, painter and musician in San Francisco and the youngest member of the Revolutionary Poets Brigade. His artistic work focuses on the queer experience and working-class struggle. He is also the creator of the Maybird Project www.themaybirdproject.com. He's organized the covers and art works for this issue, with Agneta Falk. **Charles Curtis Blackwell** is a writer, poet, playwright, and visual artist. He currently conducts writers' workshops at Youth Spirit Artworks in Berkeley, CA. California and New York are the twin poles between which **Victoria Brill** lives, moves, and has her being. Born on one, reborn on the other, she continues as a cultural worker for peace and unity. **Daniel Brooks** is a poetry editor for Unity, a charity anthology by Barrio Blues Press. His work has appeared in the Indianapolis Review, Hawai'i Review, People's Tribune, and more. **Kristina Brown** is a writer, painter, and poet. She often writes about what people will, and will not, do for love. **Neeli Cherkovski**'s most recent poetry collection Hang On To The Yangtze River has recently been adopted for poetry courses at Harper College in Chicago. **Bobby Coleman** is Managing Editor of Jambu

Press, San Francisco, and co-founder of the Revolutionary Poets Brigade. **Kitty Costello**'s collection Upon Waking: New & Selected Poems 1977-2017 gathers 40 years of her San Francisco writings. She is co-editor of the new anthology Muslim American Writers at Home: Stories, Essays & Poems of Identity, Diversity & Belonging, helping to overturn Islamophobia. **John Curl** is the author of Revolutionary Alchemy, Yoga Sutras of Fidel Castro, and Ancient American Poets. His book Indigenous Peoples Day documents the history of the new holiday, of which he is one of the founders. He translates poetry from several Indigenous languages, and is one of the editors and translators of this Anthology. **Gary S. Daniel alias Nèg Gonbolyen (Okraland Man)** hads published seven poetry books. Trilangual Press from Cambridge Massachusetts will publish his eighth, Pwezi Foutbòl 2 a 1 / Life Soccer 2 to 1 in May 2021. He has received an honorary plate from the Firefly Society's 50 years (Sosyete Koukouy) for promoting the Creole language. **Diego De Leo** came to the USA from Italy when he was 17 (he's 86). He began writing poetry 10 years after his wife died. His third book, I'm Tempted to Write a Poem, was published in the Spring of 2021. **Carol Denney** is a Bay Area musician, poet, and cartoonist, founder and editor of the Pepper Spray Times, and member of the Revolutionary Poets Brigade. **Carlos Raúl Dufflar** is Founder and Artistic Director of The Bread is Rising Poetry Collective as it celebrates 26 years, the Beat Poet Laureate for New York City, New York State for 2020-2022 and a member of the NYC RPB. **María J. Estrada** is a poet and fiction writer. She is a member of the League of Revolutionaries for a New America, Chicago. When she's not teaching college creative writing, she runs Barrio Blues Press, a charity press aimed at elevating emerging voices. **Agneta Falk** is a member of the World Poetry Movement and the San Francisco RPB. She is also a painter of international renown and is preparing her third major volume of poems for publications. She also created the cover image of this anthology and translated the poem of Bengt Berg from Swedish. Marco Fazzini b. 1962 has published seven poetry collections, and translated some of the major English and Scottish poets into Italian. His latest books are two collections of interviews with poets. He is lecturer at the University of Ca' Foscari, Venice. **Marcos Freitas** is a poet, engineer, environmental and cultural activist. He lives in Brasília and is the author of In the Coming Afternoon, among others. Member of the National Association of Writers (ANE) and Brazilian Union of Writers (UBE). **Rafael Jesús González**. Four times nominated for a Pushcart Prize, he was honored in 2015 by the City of Berkeley with a Lifetime Achievement Award. In 2017 he was named the first Poet Laureate of Berkeley. Former Earth First! Journal poetry editor and 20-year Green Party county commissioner, **Art Goodtimes** is co-director of the Telluride Institute's Talking Gourds poetry program. His latest book is Dancing on Edge: the McRedeye Poems (Lithic Press, 2019). **Adam Gottlieb** is a poet, musician, and organizer from Chicago. He is the leader of a reggae-fusion band, Adam Gottlieb and OneLove, a founding member of the Chicago Revolutionary Poets Brigade as well as the Chicago Union of the Homeless, and a writer for the People's Tribune. **Egon Günther**, b. 1953, lives as a poet and a painter in Upper Bavaria. **Lapo Guzzini** is a San Francisco-based translator, editor, and arts agitator. Until 2015 he ran The Emerald Tablet, an independent cultural venue. He's translated the poems of Sandro Sardella and Sandro Spinazzi in this issue, and is completing a book of Sardella's poetry. **Bill Hatch** is a Northern California poet and translator of poems of Roque Dalton. **Martin Hickel** thinks of himself as communist and hopes his poetry reflects that. A child of the paradise, which is the San Francisco Bay region -- he's always wondered why more people don't open their eyes. **Jack Hirschman** is an emeritus Poet Laureate of San Francisco. His latest work is a translation from Yiddish of Yitzhak Katzenelson's The Song of the Massacred Jewish People. His own fourth Arcanes will be published later in the year. He is one of the editors of this book. **Everett Hoagland** was the first Poet Laureate of New Bedford, Massachusetts, and is Emeritus Professor at UMass Dartmouth. He recently received the annual Langston Hughes Society Award and his most recent book is (the third printing of) Ocean Voices. **Marcelo Holot**, b. 1945 in Buenos Aires, is a journalist and investigative historian, and has interviewed five Nobel Laureates, Argentine and Foreign Presidents, National and Foreign Ministers and writers from Jorge Luis Borges to Jaques Cousteau, among others. He translated the Amparo Casasbellas Alconada poem, along with Doreen Stock. In the 1980s, **Bruce Isaacson** wandered into open readings in SF's North Beach. Later, he was the first Poet Laureate of Clark County, Nevada, a community of two million souls that includes the City of Las Vegas and the Las Vegas Strip. **Susu Jeffrey** grew up in the U.S. Midwest on mashed potatoes and politics. She writes about her Roma ancestry, water issues and that which outrages her. **Ziba Karbassi**, born in Iran, has lived in London from a very young age. In 2009 she was chair of Exiled Writers Ink in the United Kingdom. In 2012, Contemporary Poetics Research Centre chose her as one of the fifteen revolutionary poets in the world. **David Lerner** was a journalist, poet, and a founder of Zeitgeist Press. He published three full length collections during his life, which ended tragically in 1997. His uncollected works, A Bouquet of Nails, will be published in 2021. **Anna Lombardo**: lives in Venice, Italy as poet, translator and cultural activist. She has published four volumes of poetry and edited three anthologies. Since 2009 she has been organizing International Poetry Festivals. **Kirk Lumpkin** is a poet, spoken word & performance artist, lyricist, naturalist, and environmentalist; author of two books of poetry, In Deep and Co-Hearing and two poetry/music CDs, The Word-

Music Continuum and Sound Poems. Musician, minister, poet, California-born, granddaughter of West Indian documented and undocumented immigrants, **devorah major** was the third SF Poet Laureate. She is also a novelist, an internationally touring performer, an arts activist, and the author of 11 published books. **Elizabeth Marino** is a Chicago poet and educator, and RPB-Chicago member. Her poetry collections include the full-length Asylum, and the chaps Ceremonies and Debris. She is a Pushcart Prize nominee. **Ángel L. Martínez** is Deputy Artistic Director of The Bread is Rising Poetry Collective as it celebrates 26 years, and a member of NYC/RPB. **Karen Melander-Magoon** has published two books against the backdrop of the pandemic, A Year of Anguish: A Time for Miracles and The Earth Turns. **Sarah Menefee** is a San Francisco poet and homeless movement activist. A founding member of the League of Revolutionaries for a New America, the Revolutionary Poets Brigade and First They Came For The Homeless. One of her latest collections is Cement. **Tureeda Mikell** is an activist for holism, and a storyteller weaving blood memory into medicine. She is the co-curator of The Patrice Lumumba Anthology, 2021, and author of, Synchronicity, The Oracle of Sun Medicine, 2020, both released by Nomadic Press. For **Gail Mitchell**, words are her foundation, and making a poem is part resistance, part fury. Emmett Till sits under her breastbone. History shatters her heart and poverty is a scathing rebuke, so she writes. It's the only way she can make sense of humanity's being inhumane. **Wardell Montgomery Jr.** defines himself as an Urban Folk Poet. His poem was inspired by John Dower's book: Cultures of War. He was interviewed by Sanho Tree on CSPAN November 21, 2010. **Alejandro Murguía** is an emeritus Poet Laureate of the City of San Francisco, a renowned international poet and a founding member of the Roque Dalton Cultural Brigade. His works are published by City Lights Books. **Majid Naficy**, the Arthur Rimbaud of Persian poetry, fled Iran in

1983, a year and a half after the execution of his wife, Ezzat Tabaian in Tehran. He lives in Santa Monica. **Carmen Naranjo** (1928-2012) was a prolific novelist, short story writer, poet, and essayist, and served as Director of EDUCA (publishing house for Central American universities) and as Minister of Culture in Costa Rica. **Bill Nevins**, born 1947, moved to New Mexico in 1996. He is a poet, a reporter for national publications, a retired educator, a member of National Writers Union, the New Mexico State Poetry Society and Revolutionary Poets Brigade. **Carlo Parcelli** was Maryland Beat Poet Laureate 2017-2019, and belongs to the National Beat Poetry Foundation. **Barbara Paschke** translates from Spanish and French and is a member of the San Francisco Revolutionary Poets Brigade and the Roque Dalton Cultural Brigade. Her work has most recently appeared in Resistencia: Poems of Protest and Revolution. She translated Fernando Rendon and Carmen Naranjo for this issue. **Jerry Pendergast** is a lifelong Chicagoan, active in US-El Salvador Sister Cities, who hopes to host and co-host Open Mics again when the Covid Infection Rate goes way down. **Gregory Pond** was born in Brooklyn to Panamanian parents, has written four books of poetry, is a member of the Revolutionary Poets Brigade and facilitator of Poetically Speaking, a weekly conference-call program for seniors. He lives in San Francisco. **Dr. Jeanne Powell** is a published poet and film critic, with four books in print. She has taught in CS, UB and OLLI programs on college campuses in California. **Mike Puican**'s debut book of poetry, Central Air, was released by Northwestern Press last August. He has been a long-time board member for the Guild Literary Complex. He has taught poetry to incarcerated and formerly incarcerated individuals in Chicago. **Jörg W. Rademacher**, b. 1962 in Westphalia, Germany is the translator of the poem of Egon Günther. He is a biographer, editor and translator who composes occasional poems in three languages and has kept a journal since 1987. **Juan**

**Hernández Ramírez** has published three volumes of poetry in Nahuatl-Spanish editions, and currently resides in Xalapa. His most recent book is Tlatlatok tetl, Piedra incendiada. He is one of the most renowned poets of the Nahuatl language. **Fernando Rendón** is a poet, editor, journalist and the founder and director of both the Medellín International Poetry Festival and the World Poetry Movement. He has participated in poetry festivals all over the world and his work has been translated into more than 15 languages, including Vietnamese. **Vincent Romero** is a member of the Pueblo of Laguna in New Mexico and Diné (Navajo Nation). A poet, story teller, lecturer, and jewelry maker, he is the facilitator of A Night of Poetry at the American Indian Center [of Chicago], a monthly event, and a Lead Veteran for the AIC. **Lew Rosenbaum** is a Chicago based poet, writer, cultural worker, former bookseller, board member of the Guild Literary Complex, part of the revolutionary movement for 50 years, and founding member of the League of Revolutionaries for a New America. **Gabriel Rosenstock**, born in post-colonial Ireland, is a poet, novelist, blogger, playwright, short-story writer, essayist, translator and children's writer. Irish (Gaelic) is his literary medium of choice. A recent title is Walk with Gandhi. **Sandro Sardella** is a poet and painter from Varese in northen Italy. His poetics are innervated by the experience of factory work and the political and avant-garde movements of the 1960/70s. He read his poems at the 2012 San Francisco International Poetry Festival. **Abdus Selim**, b. 1945 received the Shaheed Munir Chowdhury 2010 award and the Lokonatya Dal Gold Medal 2019 for his contributions to Bangla theatre, and the Bangla Academy Literary Award 2015 for his translation works from English and German to Bangla, which includes poets and playwrights from Shakespeare to Brecht. **Luís Filipe Sarmento** b. 1956 in Lisbon. Poet, journalist, translator and film director. He has published over 30 books of poetry, fiction and essays. Some of his books and texts have been translated into 14 languages. **Kim Shuck** is the 7th Poet Laureate of San Francisco, emerita, and author of eight solo books. Her most recent book is Exile Heart from That Painted Horse Press. **Dinos Siotis** has published 35 books of fiction and poetry in Greek, English and French. His poems have been translated into many languages, including Arabic and Chinese. In 2011 he started Poets Circle in Athens. He is director of the Athens World Poetry Festival and the Tinos International Literary Festival and spends his time between Athens and Tinos, Greece. **Douglas Reid Skinner** was born in South Africa and has lived there and in New York, San Francisco and London. He has published poetry collections. With Marco Fazzini he was awarded joint-First Prize in the 1995 British Comparative Literature Association's Open Translation Prize. **Alessandro Spinazzi**, b. in Venice, Italy1953. Saved by Howl. Years wasted collecting records, currently an abundant poet. His works have been published by CC. Marimbo Press in Berkeley and he makes the Internet a distributing instrument of his poetry. **Doreen Stock**, a poet, literary translator, and memoir artist recently launched Bye Bye Blackbird (The Poetry Box, April, 2021), poems touching her mother's last days, and looks forward to the publication of A Noise in the Garden, selected poems forthcoming from Kelsay Press. **Matthew Talebi** immigrated to the United States from Iran in 1984, and retired as an ophthalmologist in 2016. In 2017 he began to write short socio-political poems. **Raymond Nat Turner** is a NYC poet currently Poet-in-Residence at Black Agenda Report. He's also Co-Chair of the New York Chapter of the National Writers Union (NWU). Turner has opened for such people as James Baldwin and People's Advocate Cynthia McKinney. **David Volpendesta** is an Anarchist, He is a member of Friends of Durruti, The Roque Dalton Cultural Brigade, and the San Francisco Revolutionary Poets Brigade. He is the author of Forbidden Psalms and Forbidden Psalms II, forthcoming in 2022. **Cathleen**

**Williams** is the editor of Homeward Street Journal, a newspaper sold on the streets of Sacramento by homeless vendors, and a member of the League of Revolutionaries for a New America. Socialist feminist activist **Nellie Wong** has authored several books of poetry. Editor of Talking Back Voices of Color (Red Letter Press), she dreams in jazz, bards in Hoisan American dialect, and cooks for working-class solidarity. **Andrena Zawinski**, daughter and granddaugher of steelworkers and coal miners, is an award-winning poet, veteran teacher of writing, and avid feminist. "Femicide" is from her forthcoming collection Born Under the Influence.

# REVOLUTIONARY POETS BRIGADE MISSION STATEMENT

NOW
As poets we are uniquely positioned to seize the possibilities of the time, bringing language to life and participating in the movement that is gathering as we speak...

IT'S TIME
Poetry has always been and continues to be not only the way the poet listens to his or her innermost being, but a way the spirit of the times, in its most forward-looking incarnation, is expressed and heard. And the times we're in, of crisis and the cry for transformation, particularly needs the news, as poet W.C. Williams said, "without which we die."

We say what we see: and that is the system that cannot rest until it extracts every drop from a desperate earth: capitalism. We say what we see: and that is the oppression of our class, driven to the streets and alleys of our cities, driven to the muddy fields, all because there is no profit in maintaining life and health. We are the harbingers of revolution and the awareness that underlies and drives it.

FOR THE REVOLUTIONARY POETS
In our common struggle toward freedom, each individual instinctively reaches for the best tool at hand. As artists, we have the most powerful tool of all, the ability to inspire, transform, and liberate, just in the nick of time as it happens, as the sick old ways rust, choke, sputter, and fade. Poets, those at the compressed razor-sharp edge of social thought, and all fellow artists of visionary courage, stay mindful of this historic opportunity, lead with strong revolutionary voice for all humankind to genuinely live and thrive in common spirit!

BRIGADE

Therefore, we want to create a Revolutionary Poets Brigade, to respond to the demands of the moment – provoking the future out of the confused minds of today, inspiring with the passion of the living word, in preparation for the development on a wider and larger scale of the uprising, the action that will overthrow this system of greed and exploitation.

As a network, we can be present and participate in the popular resistance that is going on around us by holding poetry events, by reading and speaking at demonstrations, and by publishing broadsides and pamphlets. Join us.

"Camerados . . . will you come travel with us? Shall we stick by each other as long as we live?"
–Walt Whitman

**REVOLUTIONARY POETS BRIGADE**
**http://revolutionarypoetsbrigade.org**

www.ingramcontent.com/pod-product-compliance
Lightning Source LLC
Chambersburg PA
CBHW020856090426
42736CB00008B/390